FUSION FLY
TYING
STEELHEAD, SALMON, AND TROUT FLIES OF THE SYNTHETIC ERA

GREG SENYO

FOREWORD BY MATTHEW SUPINSKI

Skyhorse Publishing

Visit our website at www.skyhorsepublishing.com.

10 9 8 7 6 5 4 3 2 1

Library of Congress Cataloging-in-Publication Data

Senyo, Greg.
    Fusion fly tying : steelhead, salmon, and trout flies of the synthetic era / Greg Senyo.
        pages cm
    Includes index.
    ISBN 978-1-63450-396-9 (hardcover : alk. paper)   1. Flies, Artificial.
2. Fly tying.   I. Title.
    SH451.S46 2015
    799.12'4—dc23
                                                    2015020034

Cover design by Jane Sheppard
Cover photo credit: John Miller
Interior photos: John Miller

Paperback ISBN: 978-1-5107-7557-2
Ebook ISBN: 978-1-5107-0103-8

Printed in China

To my wife Theresa and my sons Bryce and Callan for putting up with countless hours, weeks, months, and years of time spent pursuing my passions for fly tying and Great Lakes Steelhead. To my parents Greg Sr. and Sandra Ritchie for bringing me up with hunting and fishing traditions and never once steering me away from my passions and always supporting my outdoor endeavors. My brother Mike Senyo and sister Sienna Senyo for always picking up my slack. My aunt Mary Ann Boury for helping out with the kids and family while I was gone on fishing excursions. To the Village of Wayne and its Police Department for their utmost support and willingness to give me the time needed to follow through and reach my personal goals.

Last but not least to my colleagues: Mike Schultz, Patrick Robinson, Brian Doelle, Tim Hess, Dustin Mason, James Hughes, Will Turek, Cory Haselhuhn, John Clouser, Jay Wisnosky, Bobby Fragale, Justin Schallaci, Ben Barger, Josh Trammell, John Miller, Chris Willen, Jason Gregory, Eirik Vitso, Mike Schmidt, Bryan Mynes, and Mike Decoteau. My loving memory of my grandparents Harry and Helen Senyo, my uncle Mike Boury, and my brother Dylan Ritchie. Since I can no longer share my stories and passions with you in person, I will always be able to share them in spirit.

FUSION FLY TYING

CONTENTS

FOREWORD

Creativity, inspiration, and passion are attributes that are delightfully bestowed, or end up as a tragic curse to very few chosen individuals in life. They are often given down to our mortal souls and life spirit from the divine powers on high whether the bestowed likes it or not.

Passions, such as in the pursuit of excellence in the art, science, and method of fly fishing and fly tying grip a chosen few into an obsession that finds no resolve. This passion possesses those few individuals into a steady, non-conformist pursuit that has no boundaries or finality. We find those gifted few totally immersed into the wonderful world of steelhead, trout, and salmon and forever striving to go to the next level, whether it is a new approach, tactic, theory, or in Greg Senyo's case, a fanciful new fly pattern.

The passion I refer to is a virtue that can be attributed to the author of this book. His creations are deceptively simple masterpieces that fuse tradition with progressive genius. He uses original and ingenious collection of materials that create an amazing effect on both angler and prey alike.

In the end, the final creation brings on a euphoric glitter to the fly creator's eye. It is an addiction which fuels and feeds a desire for a master creator's constant need, driven by the pursuit of perfection, artistic excellence in design and function. This occurs before the fly leaves the vise and regardless of the ultimate outcome. Greg Senyo has been smitten with this never-ending passion—the 'gift or curse' of striving to 'take it up a notch' and never be satisfied with mediocrity. A new age of fusion fly design is alive and well in Greg Senyo's book, and he welcomes you on his journey.

The Great Lakes has an uncanny way of grabbing a hold of a young soul. As a young boy, I had the same epiphany along the thunderous power of Niagara Falls. Here the hydrological force of the entire Great Lakes passes through giant cascades where I would stare at the water falling in a mesmerizing trance. It was a magical place full of daredevil stories and European immigrants trying to forge a new life after a devastating world war. The fascination with fish and game was a constant draw to a young boy since there were no electronic play stations to keep one indoors. One's whole youthful life revolved around being outside, fishing, hunting, mischievous explorations and sports. Greg Senyo had that epiphany along the banks of Elk Creek near Erie, Pennsylvania, the area today known as "Steelhead Alley."

I was drawn to the local fishing bait and tackle shop, where I would dust off old bins of archaic fly patterns like Mickey Finns and Gray Ghosts. Since nobody wanted them, and I was mesmerized with the new florescent hardware technology of spoons and down-river Dodgers divers, the shop owner would give them to me for free before they began to rust. My mother would buy me fabric from the yarn shops to make my egg patterns before the globe of material came out.

Greg Senyo had a similar experience. He was so drawn to the art of fly fishing at an early age that he stole a box of flies from a tackle shop, only to be forced to give them back by his parents. Once he had his first job he got his fly tying kit. The passion was well on its way and the metamorphosis of the fly artisan was beginning to unfold.

In 2001 when my book *Steelhead Dreams* came out, Greg asked me to come to Elk Creek to give a presentation on the theory, method, science, and madness of Great Lakes steelhead fly fishing. During this appearance, I saw the gleam in Greg's eye. He sat by the fly-tying bench injecting power paint into fabric yarn to make magnificent micro egg patterns for use on the tiny steelhead streams and rivers along Lake Erie's Steelhead Alley. The ever-challenging steelhead fishery forces you to take your fly-tying game up a notch on a consistent basis and on this basis, Senyo became a master.

His fly-tying evolution came at a rapid pace. Wiggle Hex Nymphs with leatherbacks, wiggle stoneflies and baitfish streamers of every kind and nature soon began to spin off his vise.

Soon, Greg began to develop fly patterns for the Orvis Company and he invented dozens and dozens of materials for Hareline Dubbin Inc., a company of five men whose materials can be found everywhere on earth today. Each year his probing intellect challenges his own designs and he is forever inventing new materials. A textile engineer could only take notes from his inquisitive mind.

As an owner and seasonal guide for Steelhead Alley Outfitters, Greg's passion for steelhead and salmon grew to fanatical proportions. This is when swinging flies on two-handed Spey rods and switch rods started a revolution in the Great Lakes fishery. Eggs and nymph patterns were being replaced by sophisticated intruders and articulated egg-sucking leech patterns. The flash was the passion as motion without movement continued another evolution. Inspired by the Skagit school of Ward French, McCune, and McDonald, Greg took the intruder concept to a new level.

Looking for more clarity and simplicity in design, he took the Temple Dog concept pioneered by the UK and Nordic country Atlantic salmon fishermen and developed scanty predator concepts using synthetic jungle cocks and materials that resembled the natural purist world, yet incorporated the aspects of UV and polarization. It is here that simple concepts like UV Ice totally transform flies into fish-catching weapons.

In this book, you will see Greg's magic as he fuses together all these concepts as only a scientist or engineer could fully understand. Greg is the hard-working policeman who has adapted an amazing approach to presenting the fly for steelhead and salmon from the Great Lakes to any destination in the entire world where you may find such fish.

I invite you to study the patterns that Mr. Senyo has brought to the fly-fishing world, fish them, and improvise on them using your own genius and Greg's inspiration as a guide.

—Matthew Supinski
March 2015
Newaygo, Michigan

INTRODUCTION

Like many fly tiers, I had an introduction to fly tying at a very young age, but not by choice. I'd ride my bicycle to both the local bait store and fly shop every week, honestly hoping they wouldn't mind sharing a few flies from the bin. More or less, I was the nine-year-old kid looking for hand-me-downs and a free candy bar. At first they were good sports and more than happy to help me out with my weekly pillaging. But it didn't take long for the both shops to figure out my routine. So after about a month I was confronted by a gentleman at the fly shop and asked if I had yet been to the bait shop earlier? Of course I lied through my teeth, not knowing they had already spoke on the phone that morning and laughed out a plan to set me straight. As I look back, this act of kindness would forever change who I was, and set in motion a path I have not strayed from to this very day.

If you're from the Erie, Pennsylvania area or frequent the steelhead fisheries there, you know the Fly Shop Gentleman. Clyde Murray stood on the porch smoking his cigarette. He knew I flat out lied to his face. Too young for the fight or flight reaction, I was expecting him to call my father. Clyde wasn't a man of many words, but he was honest, he worked hard, and in his own right was one of the best tiers and anglers in the region. After a few minutes of pondering, he gave me an opportunity.

Instead of labeling me the "bad kid," he offered to teach me how to tie flies, and gave me the equipment I needed. I met Clyde once a week at Folly's End Fly Shop, where we would tie a different fly for hours and stock up our boxes. The education I received over the next two years would prove to be priceless.

By my early teens I was obsessed with tying. There was no such thing as one or two flies. It wasn't long before I met another young angler and someone who would become a lifelong friend in Jason Gregory. Jason lived on the bluff overlooking the river. Every day after school and every weekend we would meet up and tie flies and fish for steelhead. Jason was the more experienced tier, and as the hours melted away our fly tying sessions became almost frightening for our parents. Together we quickly started adapting to all the new materials hitting the fly shop. It's funny to think back and look at how mesmerized we were by the addition of color dyed rabbit fur and crystal flash.

We were well-oiled machines by the time we graduated high school. Soon after, we were guiding clients, and came to know the other anglers in the fly fishing arena. We started a commercial fly tying business together and supplied the local shops with the latest steelhead flies. Over the next six years it was all about trial and error and finding a path that worked well for our clients and us. Eventually we created Steelhead Alley Outfitters, a full-time outfitter in the region that is still active and strong to this day.

As fly tiers, are we really that different? Like many of you, I needed to put in many years at the vise learning and honing the techniques required to fill and complete a functional and effective fly box. There was no instant gratification, no social media, and only a basic understanding of the Internet. Perhaps like me, you wanted to learn how to tie flies because you were fascinated, entertained, and wanted to learn a skill set that allowed you to be creative without boundaries and skepticism.

Thankfully I was lucky enough to have good mentors. I took fly-tying classes just like many of you have. I formed lasting friendships with others who shared the same passion, and openly listened to every word they had to say. We studied what each tier was doing and always kept an open mind to the possibilities and personal applications obtained from these collective contributions.

Like everything else that's good in life, the process was slow but rewarding. Staying active with my tying and following the perspectives and experiences from anglers tying for fresh- and salt water was extremely beneficial. The best advice I received was to become a sponge, and absorb any tip or trick any tier was willing to share. Because I was willing to go the extra mile and not the quick road, I realized that following step-by-steps and confining to rules was never going to work with my personality. As I became more proficient at tying, I always had the urge to replace or change some, if not all of the materials, and began experimenting with my own ideas and designs. The purpose of this was more or less to address my own personal needs and to make a fly pattern functional and applicable to my fishery.

If you are a beginner that has been tying for a year or less, you should have the basic skills mastered. At this point you are probably tying a fair amount of flies. Like the majority of us, early on you struggle with certain techniques and avoid these tying conundrums like the plague. Still you are interested in tying new flies that revolve around your personality and your fisheries. At the same time you have a love affair with tradition and the roots of fly fishing's humble beginnings. You strive to be innovative and put you own special touch on your favorite foundation flies like the Woolly Bugger, Gray Ghost, Zonker, and Muddler Minnow. Now you're at the point whether you wonder if there is a better, more efficient, and easier way to tie these same flies.

If you are an advanced tier, you have mastered and learned the latest and greatest tying techniques. You have gone straight rogue and your technique is no longer the issue holding you back. Now you have become bored with repetition and simplicity. The original patterns you learned have not lost their appeal to you, but they certainly have lost their luster. Your mind constantly drifts into the experimental abyss phase of tying. You have now become your worst critic, and overly examine every fly you tie with a strict and harsh set of guidelines.

I hope with the descriptions above, I have hit on the mark what some of you are feeling and thinking about where you are in your fly tying. Please keep in mind that no matter your current skill level, or what you believe to be your achieved level, you still have room to learn. I'm constantly thinking about my tying, achieved function of the fly, and material properties that allow me to meet my expectation. I'm also willing to test them thoroughly and fail miserably. To be able to do this you must be willing to learn all tying techniques and respect the traditional base and innovative concepts that gave you the skill set to move beyond just tying a fly.

I was no longer satisfied with simplistic or conformist methods of how we should dress a fly. The past decade has seen an astronomical amount of new, exciting, and functional tying materials and components. Social media has linked fly tiers together as a collective whole, allowing us to instantly share the latest tying techniques and material applications at warp speed. Educational content that used to take months to acquire, can now be viewed with a touch of a button. Now it is all too familiar that anyone with an opinion regardless of expertise can post a photo and feel the instant gratification and self-worth for tying a fly.

The point of this book is to share a few ideas and applications you may not have seen before. To urge you to slow down, become a sponge, and take in as much information as possible. The focus is on tying flies for Steelhead, Migratory Brown Trout, and Salmon Flies. The techniques, fly patterns, and tying instructions were learned after a long road of trial and error. Hopefully you find the information valuable and applicable to the creation of your own patterns.

There are many influential tiers in our industry today. Whenever possible, I make a point to give full credit to the individual that is believed to have created or was responsible for introducing me to a certain technique or pattern. I don't claim to be the inventor of every fly pattern in this book. We each have our own very distinct styles and applications that have become our signatures and well known among our peers. At times the platform or the design of the fly may be similar, but the purpose and functionality of the fly are distinctly its owner's. It is not uncommon for species-oriented tiers from across the continent to think of, or develop similar tying concepts and pattern ideas in the same time frame. In reality this is good communication and practice between good fishermen.

My intent with *Fusion Fly Tying* is to encourage you to experiment, steer you toward adapting new materials, meld modern and traditional tying styles, and hopefully see new innovations develop from the jaws of your own vise. The goal is for you to be able to create practical, applicable, motivational, and functional flies. I sincerely want you to question the purpose of this tying. For some, you may see what I am doing as useless, or it may not fit your style or personality. It's ok to feel that way, as this book really isn't for everyone. One thing that is for certain, is that modern synthetic material, improved tying components, thought-out pattern functionality, and tier personality have created more influential flies over the past decade than ever before.

Over the years I have become acquainted with many incredible and innovative fly tiers. At the same token, I have witnessed many tiers who didn't take the time to test and think about the functionality of the fly they created or enhanced. This led to very cool and visually pleasing flies that were mediocre at best in function and purpose. With the internet, social media, and a hoard of ridiculous chat rooms and forums, we as tiers have become exposed to each other's idiosyncrasies on a daily basis.

Very little thought is taken in consideration of style, and most importantly, the intended function of a developed pattern. Fly enhancement and advancement have become replaced with straight duplication and biased opinions. You should only be critical of your own opinion and quickly be able to discuss the advantages and disadvantages of certain material applications, components, and how they can be utilized to your advantage and in your fishing applications. The only true way to do this is to investigate, experiment, and allow yourself to try something different. I can only offer my opinions and experiences, but I will support them and my tying with theory, reason, and most importantly time in the field. If nothing else I encourage you to tie them, fish them, and evaluate what works best for you.

—Greg Senyo
June 2015
Holland, Ohio

ARTIFICIAL INTELLIGENCE

I don't know a fly angler today who doesn't look forward to fishing their favorite fly. No matter where you are fishing, we all have that one ace-in-the hole pattern that provides complete confidence. This fly design holds a special place for you, and you alone. It is only fitting that this fly is the first through the sweet spot. During this process, for some mysterious reason you're casting is accurate, your line mends with ease, your heart beats faster, and your attention is focused on what will happen next. Simply tying this fly on your line gives you confidence, creates excitement, and builds up an overwhelming sense of anticipation. The A.I. or Artificial Intelligence is my confidence fly.

I needed a personal fly pattern that was completely adaptable to the harsh elements and unpredictable watersheds of the Great Lakes Region, as well as suited to the rivers of Alaska, the West Coast, and Canadian watersheds. Durability and availability were essential; today some of the finest feathers, furs, and components we use have become scarce, extremely expensive, nonexistent, or even illegal. Over the years I really began to explore and became obsessed about the creation of synthetic substitutes for my favorite natural materials. I wanted Temple dogs, Intruders, Scandinavian, and classic salmon flies. I needed them to be designed with materials I could readily find and be able to tie for my clients and friends without fear of losing every other fly to the river bottom, a boulder, or a tree branch. The A.I. was born out of this concept. Light weight and easy to cast, movement without motion, translucent, adaptable, and a confidence builder.

Most tiers and anglers only look at the flies they create on the vise, streamside, or in a bin. I use a swim tank to quickly gauge colors, translucence, and movement. I also add different ingredients to change the water viscosity. Coffee and chocolate milk are two of my favorite liquids to add into the swim tank water. This changes the water clarity and imitates the different conditions I will encounter over the course of a season while on the river. I can add different amounts of food coloring to enhance the mix as well. I adjust the lighting to simulate direct sun light, overcast, dusk, and dawn photo periods. There is no better or easier way while at your vise to visually see the contrast of your fly against water clarity conditions other than this method. This has been a valuable tool in creating contrasting patterns that perform when I get them to the river, and gives me a box full of flies that I know fish should be able to detect in adverse water.

On more than a few occasions several anglers have asked me why I use a set of four-bead chain eyes in a lot of my patterns. I first saw this concept tied by long time Michigan Guide, Kevin Feenstra. The obvious reasons are to add a little weight and balance to his flies. For the A.I., that is not the main reason. The main advantage for adding a set of four-bead chain eyes is the ability to change the A.I.'s action and movement in the river. By simply turning the fly over I can take my multi tool while on the river and cut off the eyes on one side or the other. Doing this totally changes the keel and swim angle and the A.I's action become more erratic and unpredictable, just like that of a stunned or injured baitfish.

This is also the technique I like to use as a trigger when fishing shale cuts, drop offs, and downed trees and timber that typically stack on both the outside and inside of some of the better runs. Sometimes only micro adjustments are needed, where adding more weight or using a heavier tip is not necessarily an option. Remember that bead chain comes in a variety of different sizes and a multitude of colors, so choosing the right size and color is based on the size of the river you are fishing, water speed or current, and the depth you are trying to target. All of this is important and your flies should incorporate these adjustments while tying.

By using this technique with bead chain you are not stuck with a set of dumbbell eyes that cannot be manipulated or adjusted on the fly pattern. No extra weight wrapped in the underbody of the patterns is required, and you are not forced to add weight to the line that can affect fly movement and function. I prefer to have as little weight as possible on all my fly patterns, relying on my sink tips to get me where I need. But there are many times where you need just a bit more weight and this gives me that option ready to go before I even get to the river.

The A.I. also helped curve some of the pattern problems we experienced during the winter months. I was tired of losing fishing time in late November and December during the most productive months to catch Great Lakes steelhead on a swung-fly presentation. Classic and customary patterns that use rabbit fur strips, fox furs, and marabou would freeze after a simple river walk to the next hole, or after a few casts in 20 degree air. The better option is to use Hedron's Flashabou as the wing, and constructing the A.I. primarily out of synthetic materials like Polar Chenille, Aqua Veil, Predator wrap, and Iceabou. Synthetics have the ability to shed water instantly and keep from turning into an ice cube, and even if they do freeze on you, putting the fly back in the water where it belongs instantly solves your icing problem. The A.I. eventually became an all-season pattern and a staple in my box.

FAVORITE COLOR COMBINATIONS

Since we are constructing patterns primarily with synthetics, your choices of color combinations become almost endless. This is fantastic if you are the type of angler who likes to put his or her own spin on your favorite patterns. I have narrowed it down to about a dozen color combinations that have consistently enticed grabs over the years. During the early season or the beginning of each run, I tend to stick to bait-fish color imitations that schooling steelhead and salmon have spent the summer chasing. Speckled Silver/Blue/Pearl, Speckled Gold/Green/Copper, and Speckled Silver/Rainbow/Pearl are all effective at imitating emerald shiners, shad, alewives, goby, minnows, and rainbow smolt.

As the season progresses I tend to select more natural river or camouflaged colorations, such as Speckled Copper/Gold/Black, Kelly Green/Speckled Gold/Speckled Copper, and Bronze/Gun Metal/Black. These colors imitate the baitfish populations that live in the rivers and tributaries, such as darters, dace, chub, baby suckers, sculpin, goby, crayfish, and leeches.

As winter approaches I like to switch to Speckled Copper/Orange/Pink, Speckled Gold/Blue/Purple, and Speckled Copper/Chartreuse/black … Fish are typically holding in the deeper sections of the river and not willing to go far without enticement. These color combos are all hot spotted and deliver a combination of food, fixed strike, and a visible trigger point.

When it comes to high water, I simply amplify the fluorescent colors or multi-tone the dark colors to provide the best contrast possible. I've had success both ways usually after presenting both color spectrums through the run before moving on. I hear a lot of anglers talking about when it's sunny you should fish bright flies, when it's overcast you should fish dark flies, but rarely do I come across an entire river with conditions this easy. Most of the rivers I've fished have very high cliffs and a lot of forest blanketing the river. The conditions go from cloudy to sunny a dozen times. Always experiment and try multiple colors, as there is no harm in going against the grain.

Clear water and big flashy flies are typically not spoken of in the same sentence. During low clear water periods I don't like to give up fishing the patterns I enjoy, nor do I want to make them smaller. Instead, I go to combinations that use a lot of flashabou in UV Clear/Clear/Pearl in the design. This gives translucence and the illusion of sparseness without sacrificing size and movement. I couple this wing with all natural-barred feathers and neutral colors like gray, off-white, and tan. Stealth and presentation are really the important factor in these conditions. Typically you only get a couple of casts at fish before they are alerted to your presence.

ARTIFICIAL INTELLIGENCE MATERIALS

Shank   5mm Blue Flymen Fishing Company Senyo Steelhead/Salmon Shank (25SA-23)

Thread   Purple UTC 70 or Veevus 8/0 (8V-298)

Eyes   Hareline Dubbin Inc. Small Rainbow Senyodelic Bead Chain (SBCM-306)

Wire   Hareline Dubbin Inc. Senyo Intruder Wire or Berkley Original Fused Fireline (THW-11)

Hot Spot   Hareline Dubbin Inc. Chartreuse Krystal Flash Chenille (KC-54)

Body   Hareline Dubbin Inc. UV Purple Polar Chenille or Senyo Aqua Veil Mixed Berries (SA4)

Under wing 1   Hareline Dubbin Inc. Baby Blue Lady Amherst Center Tail feather (LAC-6)

Under wing 2   Senyo's UV Barred Predator Wrap (BPW2)

Over wing 1   Grape Flashabou (FLA-6919)

Over wing 2   Sea Foam Flashabou (FLA-6929)

Over Wing 3   Gun Metal Flashabou (FLA-6916)

Hackle   Hareline Dubbin Inc. Black Schlappen Feather (SCHL-11)

Collar   Hareline Dubbin Inc. Baby Blue Strung Guinea Fowl Feather (SGF-6)

Eyes   Jungle Cock or Hareline Dubbin Inc. Real Fake Jungle Cock (FJ-5)

Hook   Partridge, Daiichi, Owner, Gamakatsu size 2–4 Intruder Style (D2557)

ARTIFICIAL INTELLIGENCE TYING INSTRUCTIONS

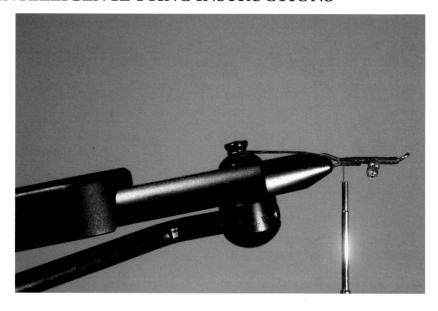

Step 1   Place a 25mm Blue Senyo Steelhead Shank from Flymen Fishing Company in your vise. Attach your UTC 70 or Veevus 8/0 thread and evenly coat the entire shank and close both front and rear loops with a thin base of thread. Cut off a 4-inch piece of Senyo's Intruder Wire or 30-pound Berkley Fireline and secure it to both sides of the shank with several thread wraps. Take the tag ends through the bottom of the front loop and fold over the top of the shank. Pull tight over the top of the shank and tie down securely with several even thread wraps. Adding glue for strength is optional. Cut off a section of four attached Senyodelic bead chain eyes and secure them with several figure eight wraps to the bottom of the shank where both wires form the front loop come together. Your wire loop length should not exceed 2 inches in total length.

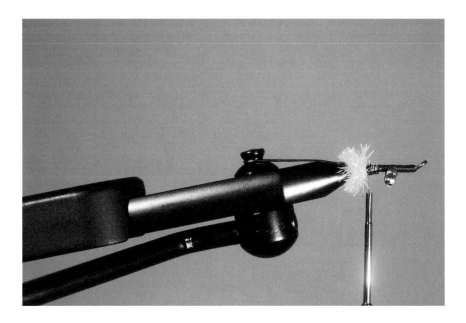

Step 2 Wind your thread back to the rear of the shank and tie in a 1-inch piece of Hareline's Chartreuse Krystal Flash Chenille. Using this chenille, make a couple tight wraps toward the front to form a small ball and secure with several more thread wraps. Make a point to use your free hand to stroke the materials toward the rear of the shank. This will help keep the chenille flowing toward the back and out of the way of your thread.

Step 3 Tie in a 3-inch piece of Senyo's Mixed Berries Aqua Veil and palmer forward toward the rear of the bead chain and secure. An easy way to get this material to work and all the fibers flowing the same direction is to get them wet and pull back tight on the fibers while you are winding forward. This will allow you to wind the material along the shank without having to wrap over existing wraps, which will increase the amount of bulk on the fly. We do not want added bulk.

Step 4   Tie in roughly twelve to twenty strands of 2-inch long Baby Blue Lady Amherst Center Tail Feather. These feathers should be tied in centered directly over the top of the polar chenille and not off to the sides and bottom. If you are like me and are not likely going to count the fibers, it's easy to remember that around ½ inch across the stem is about twenty strands.

Step 5   Take ten to twelve strands of Senyo's UV Barred Predator Wrap. The fibers cut off of the cord are roughly 4 inches long. Center tie them on top of the Lady Amherst so that the Predator wrap is just past the Amherst feather tips. Fold the remaining material over the top and secure with several thread wraps. It is important to note that I try at all cost to keep the ends of the Predator wrap uneven to give the pattern its tapered look versus a uniformal or straight-cut finish.

Step 6 Tie in twelve to fifteen strands of 5-inch long Sea Foam Flashabou over the top of the Predator wrap. The flashabou should extend roughly about ¼ inch past the predator wrap. Fold over the remaining flashabou over the top and secure with several thread wraps.

Step 7 Tie in the final selection of twelve to fifteen strands of 5-inch long Purple Flashabou over the top of the Iceabou. The Flashabou should extend roughly about ¼ inch past the last Flashabou wing. Fold over the remaining Flashabou over the top and secure with several thread wraps.

Step 8   Repeat the same process with twelve to fifteen strands of Gun Metal Flashabou and lock all the material down with several thread wraps. *Note:* While working with Flashabou as a solid wing, I tend to take each section of twelve to fifteen strands and soak them in water. As you pull them out they condense and stick together for easy tie-in without errant strands in the way. Once this is done, lay them out in a row on a paper towel for easy use. This is an easy way to prepare and prep for multiple flies and have the wings ready for a faster tying session.

Step 9   Select a good webby 5–7 inch long piece of Black Schlappen. Tie in the feather by the tip behind the Senyodelic bead chain. Palmer several wraps of schlappen behind the eyes to cover up any previous thread visible from tying in the wing, then palmer through the center of the bead chain and make several wraps to form a collar around the front of the eyes. I typically just get to the marabou section of the schlappen before securing with several thread wraps and tying off.

Step 10   Palmer a nice collar with a Baby Blue Guinea feather by tying the feather in by the tip so that the curve of the feather is facing down over top of the fly. This should look like an upside-down boat. Slowly wind the guinea toward the eye of the hook while pulling back on the feather fibers so they don't become tangled in each wrap. I typically wrap around the shank four times and tie off, but you can go thicker by adding a couple of extra wraps. If you would like a thinner profile you can also strip one side of the guinea and tie it in following the same steps.

Final   You can add a set of Jungle Cock Eyes, or a set of Hareline's Real Fake Jungle Cock. This is optional and is not required to finish off the pattern, but is preferred... I have found that fishing patterns with a very visible eye can be a trigger on predatory fish such as steelhead, salmon, and trout. *Note:* If you chose to add your eyes make sure to build a small and uniform head of thread, and coat with a slight amount of Crazy Glue. Crazy Glue is now available with a brush, allowing clean and easy application. I rarely whip finish or half hitch anymore. The glue is stronger than any knot you can tie. Your A.I. pattern should finish out around 4 inches.

2

TROPIC THUNDER

I sit at my fly tying area daily for hours at a time, spinning up the latest or hot fly patterns for customers and clients. My desk is a hideous mess of fly-tying material scraps from many tasty creatures. My floor is covered with fifty shades of dubbing, and the vacuum doesn't work because it's plugged with flashabou and intruder wire. Hooks are permanently imbedded in curious places around the room. I still can't figure out how they got there. My fingers and hands are often stained like a bag of Skittles melted on them from using Copic and Sharpie permanent markers. Clear

Cure Goo has only added to the hot mess by firmly sticking bags, coasters, markers, and fur to the table and chair. Every once in a while out of the mess you see something appear, and you instantly let loose a giant brain fart of the fly you absolutely need to tie right now. The Tropic Thunder came out of the pile of scraps to become one of the best abstract streamers I fish today. And yes, for the record this fly was made in the wee hours of the morning, with lack of sleep, and while listening to a replay of the Jack Black and Ben Stiller movie *Tropic Thunder* on TV.

Every once in a while you really need to try something different. I can't think of a natural creature that incorporates the combination of pink, orange, and chartreuse in the wild. I'm sure there is some tropical fish out there, and someone will email me a picture of Nemo the clown fish just to prove me wrong. My point is simply to draw attention, show something unique and hopefully a fish will be curious enough to follow the fly and eventually grab it. As fly fishing and tying has grown in popularity, our rivers and fish see more than a few flies over the course of a season. Sometimes fishing pressure is so high that fish can become educated rather quickly. salmon, trout, and steelhead that have felt the hook prick will start to shy away from the common color combinations we have fished for years. I like to use the Tropic Thunder especially for migratory trout, Alaskan rainbow and char, Pacific salmon, Great Lakes/PNW steelhead, and migratory smallmouth bass.

The purpose of the Tropic Thunder was to have a pattern in my arsenal that I knew no one around me would dream of fishing. It provides a spiderlike silhouette and incorporates multi-toned materials that impart a lot of wavy snake like movements in the water. The Tropic Thunder is tied sparse, hollow, and is extremely light in weight. Translucence is always a factor, and you will hear this a lot though the entire book. While long ostrich, taper-trimmed blended furs, and synthetic brushes provide the foundation for the profile of this pattern, the Clear Cure Goo UV resin applied in the final step is what really makes this fly swim and come alive.

One of the most common things I hear today from both guides and anglers, is that they tie only out of necessity, only the bare minimum, and the fastest fly they can tie, so they can be finished and back on the water. They state that it's not worth the time and effort to tie nice flies for a client or buddy who may just put the fly in a tree or stick it to the bottom of the river in a few casts. If you are this type of angler that's ok and it's not a problem, but realize I'm not this type of angler and you will not convince me otherwise.

I understand that simple flies can be extremely effective and produce fish, but I've seen the difference first hand over many years of guiding. When you open a box of flies for the first time in front of an angler the impression can go two ways. I want a potential client, a friend, or family member who is fishing with me to be excited at the prospect of catching a steelhead or salmon on my fly. Today clients spend a lot of money per day to fish with you or to purchase your flies for their fishing excursions.

I am a firm believer that the time is warranted on the vise to make sure they get what they deserve. The Tropic Thunder is one of those flies that require extra time-consuming steps. As an Abstract style pattern you don't need dozens of this fly in your box. Just a few will suffice to give you an alternative that may be extremely effective when fishing pressure is high or the bite just isn't on.

Because the Tropic Thunder is designed sparse and wispy, the pattern would simply collapse onto itself and eliminate the spider-type tentacles and movement we are trying to maintain in the river current without the addition of Loon Flow or Clear Cure Goo Resin. Once the fly is constructed, the resin is added to the center of the foxy brush underwing and allowed to settle and seep into the materials. In doing this we create a cone-shaped internal shell that will allow us to position and hold out the ostrich plumes to a desired position. As soon as you hit the resin with a UV spectrum light the resin hardens and holds its shape even under pressure from the strongest water currents and speeds. The weight of the Clear Cure Goo also gives the pattern balance, a touch of weight to create a slow sink, and a pulsating movement as it forces water over the ostrich plumes.

FAVORITE COLOR COMBINATIONS

Of the endless color combinations available I've narrowed it down to two colors that really make a difference and that are productive. These color variations did well on everything from Alaskan salmon species, particularly the king salmon to both Great Lakes and west coast steelhead, and sea-run and lake-run brown trout.

The Orange/Pink/Chartreuse color combination is most effective in watersheds that hold sediment and maintain somewhat milky brown flows that clear to a tannic color over an extended amount of time. These waters never truly clear until the river or stream is at the point where they are too low to fish a swung fly effectively. This holds true for many runoff periods after heavy rainfall where the conditions change rapidly and the river is on the drop, versus a sustained runoff that can be observed from snowmelt. The runoff can last an extended amount of time and usually the majority of the sediment has a chance to filter into the stream gradually, producing a greener, more consistent stream condition.

The Blue/Chartreuse/Purple version has been exceptional on big water containing large, deep, long runs that maintain steady, but easy-go-lucky current speeds. On the Great Lakes this has become the color combination I like to use in late winter while fishing deep, slow pools and long, slow runs. Typical water temperatures are usually around 35° F. The fly generates enough movement that no angler manipulation to further enhance the swim is needed. This color version was originally created for several guide buddies and clients swinging for big freshwater king salmon in Alaska.

TROPIC THUNDER MATERIALS

Thread   Hot Orange UTC 70 or Veevus 6/0 (6V-137)

Shank   40mm Orange Flymen Fishing Company Senyo Steelhead/Salmon Shank (40SA-271)

Wire   Senyo's Intruder Wire or Berkley Original Fused Fireline (THW-271)

Tail   Hareline Dubbin Inc. Cerise Ostrich Herl Plumes (OH-126)

Markings   Red Copic Sketch Marker (CSK-310)

Body   Hareline Dubbin Inc. Hot Orange Flat Diamond Braid (FD-271)

Rib   Veevus Medium French Gold Tinsel (VTM-153)

Underwing   EP Senyo's Copper Candy 3.0 Chromatic Brush (WSC-3)

Wing   Hareline's Orange Barred Ostrich plume piece (BP-271)

Flash   Pink Lateral Scale Flash (LSC-1765)

Collar   Hareline Dubbin Inc. Chartreuse Strung Guinea fowl feather (SGF-54)

Eyes   Jungle Cock or Hareline Dubbin Inc. Real Fake Jungle Cock eyes (FJ-5)

Hook   Partridge, Daiichi, Owner, Gamakatsu Size 2–4 Intruder Style (D2557)

Epoxy   Clear Cure Goo Tact Free UV Resin or Loon Outdoors Flow Fly Finish (LN100)

TROPIC THUNDER TYING INSTRUCTIONS

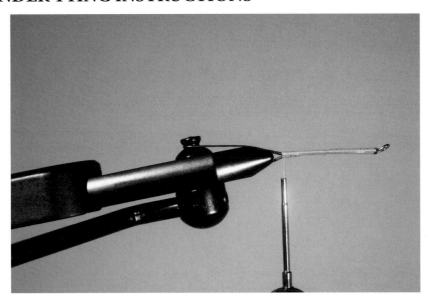

Step 1   Place a 40mm copper/orange Senyo Steelhead Shank from Flymen Fishing Company in your vise. Attach your UTC 70 or Veevus 6/0 thread and evenly coat the entire shank and close both front and rear loops with a thin base of thread. Cut off a 4-inch piece of Senyo's Intruder Wire or 30-pound Berkley Fireline and secure it to both sides of the shank with several thread wraps, forming your hook loop. Take the tag ends through the bottom of the shank eye and fold over the top of the shank. Pull tight over the top of the shank and tie down securely with several even thread wraps. Adding glue for strength is optional. Your wire loop length should not exceed 2 inches in total length.

Step 2   Wind your thread back to the rear of the shank and tie in eight cerise ostrich plumes that are roughly 2 inches long and secure all feathers on top of the shank with several thread wraps. With one hand take and pull back on the ostrich so that all plumes are tight and together. Use a permanent red Copic or Sharpie marker and make four or five evenly-spaced vertical bars across all the plumes.

Step 3   Tie in a 3-inch piece of Hareline's orange flat diamond braid and a 3-inch piece of Veevus Gold Medium French Tinsel. Evenly wrap the diamond flat braid toward the eye of the shank, stopping where the two wires are bent and meet to form the eye. Take the Gold French Tinsel and make five to six evenly-spaced wraps forward to the same point where the two wires meet and secure with several thread wraps. When tying on longer shanks and building a longer body, I like to put a thin coat of Crazy Glue over the body to prevent unwinding or damage from fish teeth.

Step 4   Take a 4-inch piece of an EP Senyo's Copper Candy 3.0 Chromatic brush and tie it in by the wire. Make four to five even wraps and secure with several thread wraps and trim away any excess materials. Take a wire brush and really comb out any of the stuck brush material.

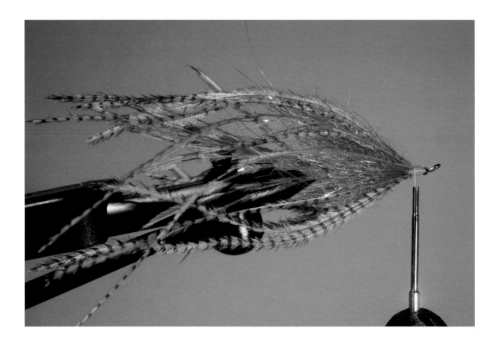

Step 5   Take six to eight plumes of Hareline's Barred Ostrich Plume Pieces roughly 4 inches long, and tie them in equally around the entire pattern. Inlay three to four strands of Pink Lateral Scale Flash to each side of the fly and make several wraps of thread to secure everything tightly in place.

Step 6   Palmer a nice collar with a Chartreuse Guinea feather by tying the feather in by the tip so that the curve of the feather is facing down over top of the fly. This should look like an upside-down boat. Slowly wind the guinea toward the eye while pulling back on the feather fibers so they don't become tangled in each wrap. I typically wrap around the shank four times and tie off, but you can go thicker by adding a couple extra wraps. If you would like a thinner profile you can also strip one side of the guinea and tie it in following the same steps.

Step 7   You can add a set of Jungle Cock Eyes, or a set of Hareline's Real Fake Jungle Cock. This is optional and is not required to finish off the pattern, but is preferred. I have found that fishing patterns with a very visible eye can be a trigger on predatory fish such as steelhead, salmon, and trout. *Note:* If you chose to add your eyes make sure to build a small and uniform head of thread, and coat with a slight amout of Crazy Glue. Crazy Glue is now available with a brush allowing clean and easy application. I rarely whip finish or half hitch anymore. The glue is stronger than any knot you can tie. Your pattern should finish out around 4–5 inches.

Final   Take your Tropic Thunder out of the vise and turn it upside down and re insert the fly into the vise by the eye of the shank. With both hands stroke all the materials down to expose the backside of the underwing. Wet your fingers and soak the tail ostrich plumes to get them to stand up together and out of the way. Grab your bottle of Tack Free UV Clear Cure Goo or Loon's Fly Finish Flow and make sure the little metal tube applicator is screwed onto the bottle. Starting at the base of the body squeeze a small bead of resin on the fox directly around the base of the body. Do not make the bead too large or too thick as it will make the glue base too wide and affect the overall action of the fly. The glue base should be no wider than a pea. Allow the UV resin to soak into the fox fibers and down in toward the thread head. You may need to lightly pull down on the wing to get the glue to start seeping. Once this is done hit the base with a UV spectrum light for roughly ten seconds and remove from the vise. You will immediately see the flare generated by the hardened Clear Cure Goo. The movement and swim action this creates is amazing and the durability is unmatched and well worth the extra time involved in creating this fly pattern.

3

PREDATOR SCANDI

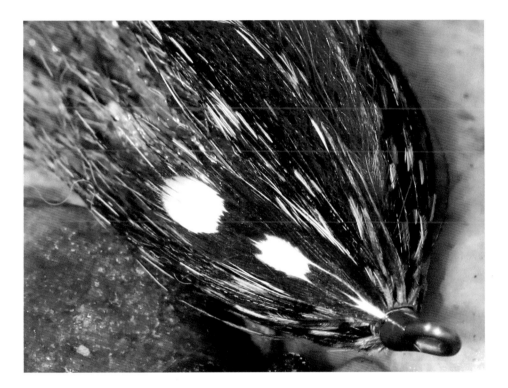

The Predator Scandi is based on the simple and beautiful Temple Dog and Scandinavian-style salmon flies. I have a love affair with this type of tying, but rarely do I have all the awesome furs needed to construct them at my disposal. In addition, I want the ability to tie this pattern with much less material, more synthetic translucence, but still maintain the teardrop profile that is so appealing to the angler, and to the fish as well. The rigid-built fox and synthetic-brush underwing of this fly allows you to use a single fur to build the entire over wing. This translates into a long and very soft fur that is free to move with minimal effort in the river current. This also forms the top of your teardrop while the trailing wing fibers emulate a short pulsating action in the water. The design's purpose is to imitate a small baitfish and maintain this profile with a lot less of the erratic movements and motion seen on some of my other patterns.

The fluoro fibre tail is built to assist the over wing but also gives the fly a hot-spotted visible lateral line that is a focused strike point for steelhead, salmon, and trout. This fly is also virtually weightless, so casting this pattern is a breeze as the synthetics cast off the majority of the water due to non-absorption. My favorite part of the Predator Scandi is that it requires little effort and time tie the fly. This is a great-looking and functional fly, and with good material-prepping practices you can fill your box with a good selection in no time.

I can't count the number of times when I have been standing on a section of stream, and trying hard to be patient with a fish that is bumping and nipping at my fly. I do my best to feel the weight of the fish before setting the hook home. If you are anything like me you probably prematurely set on a number of fish before you got that commitment. It happens to us all and honestly I like knowing that a fish can still get me excited into making those mistakes.

I like to fish large patterns because I crave that moment the fish has finally decided to surrender, and allows me to slowly bring them to hand. Seeing that giant fly swimming off the side of chromed-out steelhead is as powerful a drug for me as the tug from the beast himself. Sometimes when I am getting continual bumps from fish, but failing to connect, changing the profile shape and contrast of a pattern like the Predator Scandi will almost always close the deal. This fly has become the primary closer for me on so many nipping fish over the years. I tie them to imitate all the colors of my larger patterns; this makes switching flies on active fish fast and easy. Having the ability to come back through with your flies and show a totally different profile of similar color schemes has greatly increased my ability to catch a number of picky fish.

I like to think of the Predator Scandi like a dart, and impart a lot of artificial movement by hand and with the rod by jigging the rod tip and making short strips. I want the short, forward-and-backward darting motion of a small fish fighting its way through the current. When I know a steelhead or salmon is active on the fly, I really like to speed up the process by throwing downstream mends. This leaves little time for the fish to make a decision about whether to take. Most strikes are pretty violent when I get to play the game this way. When a fish gets hung up or is only willing to travel so far, I slow it down by putting in an upstream mend. On this mend I strip the fly faster and allow it to drop back into the zone on slight pauses in the strip to entice a strike. The Predator Scandi is especially good for migratory and resident trout, Alaskan rainbow and char, Pacific salmon, and Great Lakes/Pacific Northwest steelhead. I favor Orange/Pink/Gold, Lavender/Blue/Pearl, Black/Purple/Pink, and Olive/Chartreuse/Copper colors.

PREDATOR SCANDI MATERIALS

Thread   Purple UTC 70 or Veevus 8/0 (U70-380)

Shank   40mm Pink Flymen Fishing Company Senyo Steelhead/Salmon Shank (40SA-289)

Loop   Senyo's Intruder Wire or Berkley Original Fused Fireline (THW-11)

Tag   Hareline Silver Flat Diamond Braid (FD-344)

Tail   H2O Products Hot Pink Fluoro Fibre (FLF-16)

Body   Hareline Purple Flat Diamond Braid (FD-298)

Rib   Veevus Gold Medium French Tinsel (VTM-153)

Under Body   EP Senyo's Purple Rain Chromatic Brush 1½ inches (SCB-13)

Under Wing   Hareline Dubbin Inc. Senyo's UV Barred Predator Wrap (BPW2)

Wing   Heritage Angling Purple Silver Fox or Hareline Dubbin Inc. Purple Arctic Fox Tail (AFT-298)

Flash   Pearl Lateral Scale or Standard Pearl Flashabou (LSC-1703)

Collar   Hareline Dubbin Inc. Lavender Strung Guinea Fowl feather (SGF-200)

Eyes   Jungle Cock or Hareline Dubbin Inc. Real Fake Jungle Cock Eyes (FJ-5)

Hook   Partridge, Daiichi, Owner, Gamakatsu size 2–4 Intruder Style (D2557)

PREDATOR SCANDI TYING INSTRUCTIONS

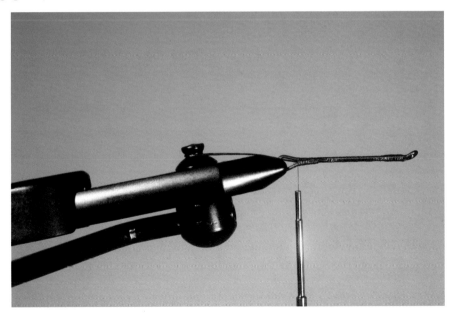

Step 1   Place a pink 40mm Senyo Steelhead Shank from Flymen Fishing Company in your vise. Attach your UTC 70 or Veevus 8/0 thread and evenly coat the entire shank and close both front and rear loops with a thin base of thread. Cut off a 4-inch piece of Senyo's Intruder Wire or 30-pound Berkley Fireline and secure it to both sides of the shank with several thread wraps. Take the tag ends through the bottom of the front loop and fold over the top of the shank. Pull tight over the top of the shank and tie down securely with several even thread wraps. Adding glue for strength is optional. Your wire loop length should not exceed 2 inches in total length.

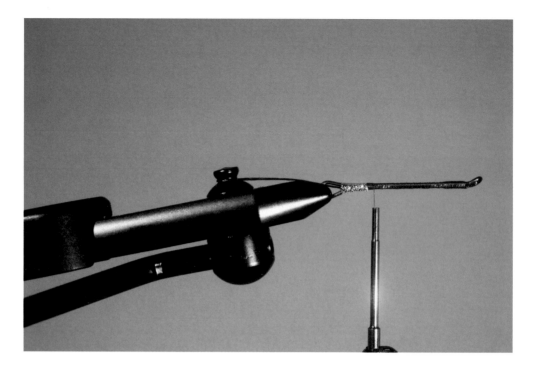

Step 2   Wind your thread back to the rear of the shank and tie in a 1-inch section of Silver flat Diamond braid. Wrap the flat braid forward until it covers the section of the shank where the two wires meet and secure with several thread wraps.

Step 3   Next tie in a section of hot pink Fluoro Fibre that is roughly 2 inches long and secure all fibers on top of the shank with several thread wraps. With one hand take and pull back on the Fluoro Fibre so that it is tight and together. Hold the fibers at a rough 45-degree angle and place a drop of Crazy Glue at the base. Allow the glue to soak up the strands and start to dry before releasing.

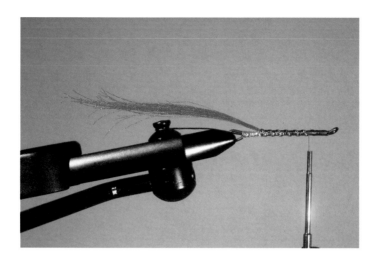

Step 4   Tie in a 3-inch piece of purple flat diamond braid and a 3-inch piece of Veevus medium gold French tinsel. Evenly wrap the mini flat braid toward the eye of the shank stopping where the two wires are bent and meet to form the eye. Take the oval French tinsel and make five or six evenly-spaced wraps forward to the same point where the two wires meet and secure with several thread wraps. When tying on the longer shanks and building a longer body I do like to put a thin coat of Crazy Glue over the body to prevent unwinding or damage from fish teeth.

Step 5   Tie in a 4-inch piece of an EP Senyo Purple Rain Chromatic 1½-inch brush, and then take a 4-inch piece of Senyo's UV Barred Predator wrap and lay it on a flat surface. Make sure all the predator wrap strands are not tangled and flowing in the same direction. Take your scissors and starting at the bottom cut a taper from 1–3 inches. This will basically look like an upside down half of a triangle. Tie in the prepped brush with the fibers all flowing toward the rear of the shank. You can bend the brush to resemble a reverse letter "L" and tie it in by the small bend. Next you tie in the Predator wrap the same way with the fibers flowing toward the rear and by the short end of the taper. Take a Copic or Sharpie marker and color the white cord of the Predator wrap purple to match the brush color. Pull up tight on both the predator wrap and the brush. Wet and stoke the fibers of both materials toward the rear with a little bit of water on your fingers, and start wrapping forward the two materials in unison. After four to five wraps you should secure

with several thread wraps and trim away any excess materials. Take a wire brush and lightly comb out any stuck materials.

Step 6   Take a clump of Hareline's purple arctic fox tail that is roughly 3–4 inches long, and tie in centered and over the top of the pattern. Do not remove the guard hairs from the fur during this step. Take three individual strands of Pearl Lateral Scale Flashabou and center tie them in on the top of the wing. Fold over the Flashabou and secure with several thread wraps. Try to keep all the lengths of the flash uneven. This is so the flash will taper and reflect at different lengths and just doesn't come to a straight line. Inlay three to four strands of Mirage Flash on top of the fly and make several wraps of thread to secure everything tightly in place.

Step 7   Palmer a nice collar with Hareline Dubbin Inc. Lavender Guinea feather, by tying the feather in by the tip so that the curve of the feather is facing down over top of the fly. This should look like an upside-down boat. Slowly wind the guinea toward the eye while pulling back on the feather fibers so they don't become tangled in each wrap. I typically wrap around the shank four times and tie off, but you can

go thicker by adding a couple extra wraps. If you would like a thinner profile you can also strip one side of the guinea and tie it in following the same steps.

Step 8   You can add a set of Jungle Cock Eyes, or a set of Hareline's Real Fake Jungle Cock. This is optional and is not required to finish off the pattern, but is preferred... I have found that fishing patterns with a very visible eye can be a trigger on predatory fish such as steelhead, salmon, and trout. *Note:* If you chose to add your eyes make sure to build a small and uniform head of thread, and coat with a slight amount of Crazy Glue. Crazy Glue is now available with a brush allowing clean and easy application. I rarely whip finish or half hitch anymore. The glue is stronger than any knot you can tie. Your pattern should finish out around 3½–4 inches.

4

THE FLOW RIDER

This is my B-52 bomber! If there is stain and leaves in the water coupled with heavy flows, this fly is cleared for takeoff. The Flow Rider is a spinoff of a Scandinavian up wing and Ed Ward's Intruder. The styles have mated and its offspring has the swim attitude that is perpetually stuck in its terrible twos! I tie this both as a single and articulated double using multiple shanks. The movement is like a heavy metal guitarist head banging on stage, it's constantly moving and refuses to stop, and it's violent and cocky swim attitude set the tone.

In October I start to anticipate and watch the forecast of the coming cold rain. As soon as it arrives, and the rivers are swollen, I wait for the flush and the flows to drop. I try to time it perfectly and get to those first couple miles of my favorite Estuaries and rivers descending into the lake. The chance for my first fish of the new season is too great to pass up. Steelhead, salmon and the brown trout are always on the prowl and still in their habits of reckless abandonment on bait. It's an exciting time to be a fly fisher and about as good as it gets.

During these early periods, I always found myself staring at the gear guys who threw Little Cleo spoons and double jointed Rapalas. These guys were constantly successful because they were taking advantage of fresh fish that spent the last five months gorging themselves on 4-inch Emerald Shiners, Shad, and a multitude of other baitfish balls in the lake. I decided to take part in the chase and tied imitations that imitated the wobble of the spoon and the wiggle of the Rapala.

Autumn is the time of the year to take advantage of fish that have not seen a fly in several months. They have the feed bags on and are willing to attack and consume offerings that are consistent with the 4–6 inch bait found in the rich inland oceans of the Great Lakes. Typically, early in the year the rivers are still full of sediment and hold color longer. This will remain consistent until adequate precipitation flushes out the summer muck. These river conditions create the same security and comfort steelhead, salmon, and trout have enjoyed all summer. Targeting their aggression and taking advantage of their sense of safety is a highly effective way to put fish on the end of your line.

By now you must have noticed that I have a base platform for many of my flies. Again, I use the bead chain under the front wing to give me the preference of changing the action of the fly on the river with a simple snip from my pliers. The long front and rear wings of the Flow Rider do not need weight for balance, as the water friction against them alone will keep this pattern riding upright and true.

Some of you will look at this fly and say that it is way too big. What you're failing to see is that this pattern, while it maintains a large profile, it also remains extremely light in weight, as it is tied hollow and very sparse. Water absorption while swimming and water shedding during casting combine for functionality within the same fly. The goal of the Flow Rider is to be able to swim a large fly, and still be able to pull it from the water and cast it effectively.

Target Species   Migratory and resident trout, Alaskan rainbow and char, Pacific salmon, Great Lakes/ PNW steelhead, and migratory pike

Favorite Colors   Orange, Olive, Blue, White, Black, Pink, and Purple

Specialty combinations   Classic Gray Ghost, Black Ghost, and Green Butt Skunk

FLOW RIDER MATERIALS

Thread   Olive UTC 70 or Veevus 8/0 (8V-263)

Shank   40mm Chartreuse Flymen Fishing Company Senyo Steelhead/Salmon Shank (40SA-54)

Connection   Senyo's Intruder Wire or Berkley Original Fused Fireline (THW-54)

Tail   H20 Products Chartreuse Fluoro Fibre (FLF-13)

Under wing   Hareline Dubbin Inc. Olive Strung Guinea Fowl Feather (SGF-263)

Over wing   Heritage Angling Olive Silver Fox or Hareline Dubbin Inc. Olive Arctic Fox Tail (AFT-263)

Flash   Speckled Copper Flashabou (FLA-6934)

Rear Collar   Hareline Dubbin Inc. Minnow Gray Silver Pheasant Body Feather (SPF-234)

Body   Lagartun Chartreuse Mini Braid or Hareline Dubbin Inc. Chartreuse Flat Diamond Braid (FD-54)

Rib   Veevus Medium Gold French Tinsel (VTM-153)

Under wing 2   Hareline Dubbin Inc. Olive Strung Guinea fowl Feather (SGF-263)

Weight   Hareline Dubbin Inc. Small Gold or Silver Bead chain (BCM-153)

Over wing 2   Heritage Angling Olive Silver Fox or Hareline Dubbin Inc. Olive Arctic Fox Tail (AFT-263)

Flash   Speckled Copper Flashabou (FLA-6934)

Collar   Hareline Dubbin Inc. Minnow Gray Silver Pheasant Body Feather (SPF-234)

Eyes   Hareline Dubbin Inc. Real Fake Jungle Cock or jungle cock (FJ-5)

Hook   Partridge, Daiichi, Owner, Gamakatsu size 2–4 Intruder Style (D2557)

FLOW RIDER TYING INSTRUCTIONS

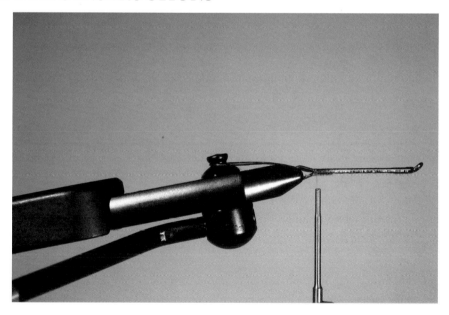

Step 1   Place a 40mm Chartreuse Senyo Steelhead Shank from Flymen Fishing Company in your vise. Attach your UTC 140 or Veevus 8/0 thread and evenly coat the entire shank and close both front and rear loops with a thin base of thread. Cut off a 4-inch piece of Senyo's Intruder Wire or 30-pound Berkley Fireline and secure it to both sides of the shank with several thread wraps. Take the tag ends through the bottom of the front loop and fold over the top of the shank. Pull tight over the top of the shank and tie down securely with several even thread wraps. Adding glue for strength is optional. Your wire loop length should not exceed 2 inches in total length.

Step 2   Palmer a nice rear collar with an Olive Guinea feather, by tying the feather in by the tip so that the curve of the feather is facing down over top of the fly. This should look like an upside-down boat. Slowly wind the guinea toward the eye while pulling back on the feather fibers so they don't become tangled in each wrap. I typically wrap around the shank four times and tie off, but you can go thicker by adding a couple extra wraps. If you would like a thinner profile you can also strip one side of the guinea and tie it in following the same steps.

Step 3   Take and cut off a section of Fluoro Fibre that is roughly 2 inches long and secure all fibers on top of the shank with several thread wraps. With one hand take and pull back on the Fluoro Fibre so that it is tight and together. Hold the fibers at a rough 45 degree angle and place a drop of Crazy Glue at the base. Allow the glue to soak up the strands and start to dry before releasing.

Step 4   Directly after the Fluoro Fibre tail, Palmer another nice rear collar with Minnow Gray Silver Pheasant feather, by tying the feather in by the tip so that the curve of the feather is facing down over top of the fly. This should look like an upside-down boat. Slowly wind the feather toward the eye while pulling back on the feather fibers so they don't become tangled in each wrap. I typically wrap around the shank four times and tie off, but you can go thicker by adding a couple extra wraps. If you would like a thinner profile you can also strip one side of the guinea and tie it in following the same steps.

Step 5   Take a clump of Hareline's Olive Arctic Fox Tail that is roughly 3–4 inches long and tie in centered and over the top of the pattern. Do not remove the guard hairs from the fur during this step. Take three individual strands of Speckled Copper Flashabou and center tie them in on the top of the wing. Fold over the Flashabou and secure with several thread wraps. Try to keep all the lengths of the flash uneven. This is so the flash will taper and reflect at different lengths and just doesn't come to a straight line.

Step 6   Attach a 3-inch piece of Chartreuse Diamond Flat braid and a 3-inch piece of Veevus Medium Gold French tinsel in front of the collar and secure. Evenly wrap the flat braid toward the eye of the shank stopping where the two wires are bent and meet to form the eye. Take the Gold French Tinsel and make five or six evenly-spaced wraps forward to the same point where the two wires meet and secure with several thread wraps. When tying on the longer shanks and building a longer body I like to put a thin coat of Crazy Glue over the body to prevent unwinding or damage from fish teeth. Attach a set of four silver bead chain eyes to the bottom off the shank where the front two wires meet to form the shank eye and secure with several figure eight thread wraps. You can add a drop of super glue to the middle of the eyes for added strength.

Step 7   Select a good webby Olive Guinea Feather and tie in the feather by the tip behind the Silver bead chain. Palmer several wraps behind the eyes to cover up any thread from tying the wing, then palmer through the center of the bead chain and make several wraps to form a collar around the front of the eyes. I typically get six or seven wraps of Guinea wrapped around, and in front of the eyes. This gives just enough bulk to hold the wing profile upright.

Step 8   Take a clump of Hareline's Olive Arctic Fox Tail that is roughly 3–4 inches long, and tie in centered and over the top of the pattern. Do not remove the guard hairs from the fur during this step. Take three individual strands of Speckled Copper Flashabou and center tie them in on the top of the wing. Fold over the Flashabou and secure with several thread wraps. Try to keep all the lengths of the flash uneven. This is so the flash will taper and reflect at different lengths and just doesn't come to a straight line.

Step 9   Palmer a nice collar with Minnow Gray Silver pheasant feather, by tying the feather in by the tip so that the curve of the feather is facing down over top of the fly. This should look like an upside-down boat. Slowly wind the feather toward the eye while pulling back on the feather fibers so they don't become tangled in each wrap. I typically wrap around the shank four times and tie off, but you can go thicker by adding a couple extra wraps. If you would like a thinner profile you can also strip one side of the guinea and the tie it in following the same steps.

Step 10   You can add a set of Jungle Cock Eyes, or a set of Hareline's Real Fake Jungle Cock. This is optional and is not required to finish off the pattern, but is preferred. I have found that fishing patterns with a very visible eye can be a trigger on predatory fish such as steelhead, salmon, and trout. *Note:* If you chose to add your eyes make sure to build a small and uniform head of thread, and coat with a slight amount of Crazy Glue. Crazy Glue is now available with a brush allowing clean and easy application. I rarely whip finish or half hitch anymore. The glue is stronger than any knot you can tie. Your pattern should finish out around 3½–4 inches.

5

GANGSTER INTRUDER

I can already imagine the eyes of traditional fly tiers the minute they look upon this pattern. They will question whether this is going to be classified as a lure or fly? The answer is simple. Yes, I tied it and it does conform to all regulations for fly fishing–only waters. The next question typically asked is, "What's the point of adding a small Indiana blade to this fly pattern?"

Going fishing these days is no small undertaking. I'm just like most of you. I've got multiple responsibilities, a family life, multiple jobs, and a business to run. It's not like the good old days when I could wake up and just decide to go fishing. Today, I have to take advantage of every possible opportunity regardless of weather and river conditions. Most of the time the weather is never on my side and I am often stuck fishing swollen and dirty rivers.

After fishing those unfriendly conditions, and having success only on a few occasions, I found myself thinking back to my teens, when I threw spinners in these very same circumstances. Although I was consistently successful back then, I knew far less about river conditions and fish behavior. I had to stop for a minute and observe how I had taken a step backward, and decided that some experimenting at the vise was necessary.

I found that by adding a very small blade to the rear loop of my steelhead shank, I could add vibrations that steelhead, trout, or salmon could feel. The blade doesn't spin at all, but instead wobbles and hits off the side of the shank creating noise and a solid reflection. By adding a set of long rubber legs and the addition of Senyo's Shaggy Dub, I am able to increase the amount of movement and vibration. I fished the Gangster Intruder the day following my first experiment with the fly, and in the same muddy conditions as the day before. I hit the same water, and fished the same runs. The only difference this time was I hit pay dirt pretty consistently.

Target Species   Migratory and resident trout, Alaskan rainbow and char, Pacific salmon, Great Lakes/PNW steelhead, and migratory pike

Favorite color combinations   Including, but not limited to Gold/Copper/Tan, Chartreuse/Gold/Black, Blue/Silver/White, and Pink/Copper/Orange.

GANGSTER INTRUDER MATERIALS

Shank   Flymen Fishing Company Black 25mm Senyo Steelhead/Salmon Articulated Shank (25SA-11)

Blade   #0 Gold Indiana blade

Wire   Senyo's Intruder Wire or Berkley Original Fused Fireline (THW-11)

Thread   Olive UTC 140 or Veevus 8/0 (8V-263)

Butt   Senyo's Pink Lady Fusion Dub (FUS10)

Tail   Hareline Dubbin Inc. Olive Lady Amherst Tail Feather (LAC-263) and Pearl Lateral Scale (LCS-1703)

Body   Hareline Dubbin Inc. UV Silver Polar Chenille (PCUV-344)

Wing 1   Hareline Dubbin Inc. Olive Lady Amherst Center Tail Feather (LAC-263)

Wing 2   Hareline Dubbin Inc. White Ostrich Herl Plumes (OH-377) and Opal/Silver Mirage (FLA-3301)

Wing 3   Hareline Dubbin Inc. White Ostrich Herl Plumes (OH-377), and Opal/Silver Mirage (FLA-3301)

Rubber Legs   Hareline Dubbin Inc. Clear Silver Metallic Rubber Legs (CL-344)

Gills   Senyo's Shaggy Dub Red (SSD-310)

Eyes   Hareline Dubbin Inc. Small Chartreuse Tungsten Predator Eyes (TPS-54)

Head   Hareline Dubbin Inc. Olive Arctic Fox Zonker Strip (AZ-263)

Throat   Senyo's Silver Minnow Belly Laser Dub (SL-352)

Hook   Partridge, Daiichi, Owner, Gamakatsu Size 2–4 Intruder Style (D2557)

GANGSTER INTRUDER TYING INSTRUCTIONS

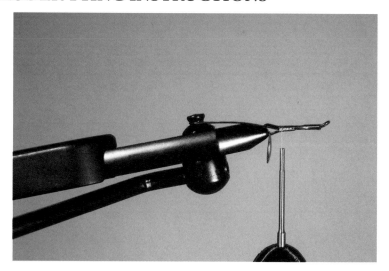

Step 1   Slide a #0 gold Indiana blade into the rear loop of a 25mm Black Senyo Steelhead Shank from Flymen Fishing Company in your vise. Attach your UTC 140 or Veevus 8/0 thread and evenly coat the entire shank and close both front and rear loops with a thin base of thread. Cut off a 4-inch piece of Senyo's Intruder Wire or 30-pound Berkley Fireline and secure it to both sides of the shank with several thread wraps. Take the tag ends through the bottom of the front loop and fold over the top of the shank. Pull tight over the top of the shank and tie down securely with several even thread wraps. Adding glue for strength is optional. Your wire loop length should not exceed 2 inches in total length.

Step 2   Take a small clump of Pink Lady Fusion Dubbing and with both hands pull it apart to get the fibers all flowing in the same direction. Take the Fusion dub and make two equal clumps and then place the together to form a small "V" in your fingers. Come over the top of the shank and place the V of the dub downward and secure the dubbing with several lose wraps in the center. This will cause the material to naturally spin around the shank evenly. Fold the front half of the material over top of itself and forcefully brush out any lose fibers. Bring your tying thread to the front of the dubbing ball and make several more wraps to lock it in.

Step 3   Take and trim off six to eight strands of 3–4 inch Lady Amherst tail feather and tie it in over top of the dubbing ball. Add ten to fifteen strands of uneven Pearl Lateral Scale flash over the Lady Amherst Tail feathers and secure with several thread wraps.

Step 4   Tie in a 3-inch piece of Hareline's UV Silver Polar Chenille, and palmer the polar chenille toward the front of the shank, making sure the fibers all lay toward the rear of the shank. If you have issues with the materials wanting to fold forward, take and wet the polar chenille with water and pull backward firmly with your fingers while winding the polar chenille around the shank. You should stop and secure the polar chenille just before the point where the shank wires meet and form the eye.

Step 5   To build the wing you will need to tie in eight to ten pieces of Olive Lady Amherst tail feather, then add five to six plumes of White Ostrich Herl Plumes. On top of that an additional ten to fifteen strands of Mirage Opal/Silver Flashabou, plus ten more plumes of White Ostrich Herl. Finish the wing off with fifteen more strands of Opal/Silver Mirage Flashabou. I understand it seems like a lot, but the blending gives the fly incredible movement, contrast, and profile.

Step 6   Rotate the fly on its belly and tie in a size small Chartreuse Tungsten Predator dumbbell eye and secure with several figure eight thread wraps. Next add a set of 3-inch long Rubber Legs to each side of the wing and secure with several firm thread wraps.

Step 7   While the fly is still belly up, take a small clump of Red Shaggy Dub, and center tie it behind the dumbbell eyes. You will follow the same steps we did to create the dubbing ball in the beginning of the fly, by pruning and placing the "V" down over the shank and center tying. Fold the remaining shaggy dubbing over itself and secure. Do not over trim the Red Shaggy Dub it is meant to be bushy. To finish the fly tie in a small clump of Senyo's Silver Minnow Belly Laser Dubbing in front of the dumbbell eyes and then bring the fly back to its upright position. Next, secure a sparse clump of Olive Arctic Fox Fur and tie it in on top and in front of the dumbbell eyes. Brush out any loose fibers in the head, and pull all the material back and create an even thread head. Add a little Crazy Glue and cut the thread.

6

THE SLIM SHADY

I have to be a little bit up front here, and tell you exactly what prompted going mostly synthetic on this next fly. See, I used to be a huge fan of Steven Tyler and Aerosmith. I mean who hasn't sung out loud to "Janie's Got a Gun"? You're already thinking about singing it. Look, it was really annoying to see all those awesome hackle feathers end up on about a million different heads after a season of "The Biggest Loser." I'm sorry I meant to say "American Idol," but it doesn't matter. The reality of what happened is not in the television show; it's in the almost instantaneous shortage of hackle for all anglers, country wide! The demand for premium hackle was so high at one point; I even sold every neck I had to the local salon for an insane amount of money.

The point of all this is that we do take for granted that many of the natural materials we use today will always be available and affordable. The truth is you cannot grow or produce enough natural material to supply a boom of this type of demand. Hackle prices unfortunately will never be the same and it has taken over a year for the fad to die down enough for a simple feather to make a comeback. I feel I was lucky during this debacle; I'd already made a choice to spend more time using manufactured materials. But for many tiers the loss of a natural material that is incorporated into their tying style and for so many of their patterns, it left little choice but to find a suitable substitute, or to forget about it all together.

Each fly tier that I have met over the years always seemed to have his or her own motivation or reasoning to tie a fly. For some it has been to save money. A few always like to paint by the numbers, and tie out of necessity. For others, it's to catch a fish on their own work, while many just love the history and art of it all. I'm always fascinated when I run into the tier who says that says they are always curious about what they can get away with. You can almost always see that half broken light bulb still flickering on top of his head, and there is much to be gained from the thinking fly tier!

The good thing about tying the Slim Shady is you are likely to never run out of the materials needed to this fly. The only thing that can happen to the materials used is that they will most likely have an upgrade in the future; 90 percent of the materials are synthetics! The Slim Shady is very durable and can take a season-long beating. The platform of this fly is based off of Ed Ward's Intruder, which is our generation's Woolly Bugger, as the endless designs, ideas, and creations spurred from Ward's Intruder have rivaled the popularity of and versatility of that venerated old fly. Whether Ed would accept this or not, it doesn't change the Intruder's place in history.

Though it appears to have a lot of flash out of water, it's underwater where this pattern really shines. Believe it or not this is a pattern I love to use in clear- to lightly-stained water, where fast current and a lot of structure exist. Once this fly is submerged it becomes almost opaque with hints of flash as it moves quickly through the current. Generally, I don't fish a pattern like this in slow-moving pools where fish have a lot of time to inspect the fly. I really want to focus on those overlooked buckets and fast-water runs, where I can present a highly visible fly very quickly across each section of water. This usually entices the fish to react quickly or not at all. Takes are typically very aggressive and happen early, as the fly turns and starts to swim against the current.

Target Species   Migratory trout, Alaskan rainbow, char, and salmon, and Great Lakes steelhead

Favorite Color Combos   Blue, Pearl, Purple, Rainbow, Copper, etc.…So when it comes to color selections, I must say this is one of the best things about using Flashabou as a winging material. Your choices of colors are limitless; you can mix and match until your heart's content. Sure I do have favorite color combinations, but in truth it's based on fishery or just always wanting to throw odd colors together to see what reaction I can get from the fish.

SLIM SHADY MATERIALS

Shank   40mm Black Flymen Fishing Company Senyo Articulated Steelhead/Salmon Shank (40SA-11)

Thread   UTC 70 or Veevus 8/0 Peacock Blue (U70-283)

Wire   Purple Senyo Intruder Trailer Hook Wire or Berkley Original Fused Fireline (THW-298)

Hot Butt   Hareline Dubbin Inc. Shrimp pink Krystal Flash Chenille (KC-343)

Rear Collar   Enrico Puglisi Purple 1.5 Short EP Foxy Brush (FXS-298)

Rear Wing   Pink Lateral Scale (LSC-1765)

Rear Collar   Hareline Dubbin Inc. Lavender Guinea Feather (SGF-200)

Body   Lagartun Lilac French Braid or Hareline Dubbin Inc. Purple Flat Diamond Braid (FD-298)

Weight   Senyodelic Rainbow Bead Chain (SBCM-306)

Bump   Hareline Dubbin Inc. Shrimp pink Krystal Flash Chenille (KC-343)

Fore Hackle   Enrico Puglisi Purple 1.5 Short EP Foxy Brush (FXS-298)

Wing   Grape Flashabou (FLA-6919) and Pink Lateral Scale (LSC-1765)

Lateral line   Senyo's Smolt Blue Wacko Hackle (WH-359)

Collar   Hareline Dubbin Inc. Lavender Guinea Feather (SGF-200)

Eye   Jungle Cock or Hareline Dubbin Inc. Real Fake Jungle Cock (FJ-5)

Hook   Partridge, Daiichi, Owner, Gamakatsu size 2–4 Intruder Style (D2557)

SLIM SHADY TYING INSTRUCTIONS

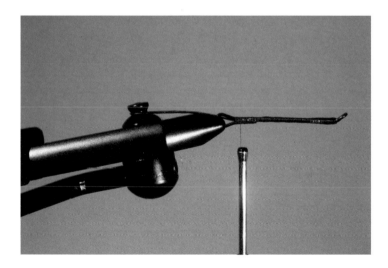

Step 1   Place a Black 40mm Senyo Steelhead Shank from Flymen Fishing Company in your vise. Attach your UTC 70 or Veevus 8/0 thread and evenly coat the entire shank and close both front and rear loops with a thin base of thread. Cut off a 4-inch piece of Senyo's Intruder Wire or 30-pound Berkley Fireline and secure it to both sides of the shank with several thread wraps. Take the tag ends through the bottom of the front loop and fold over the top of the shank. Pull tight over the top of the shank and tie down securely with several even thread wraps. Adding glue for strength is optional. Your wire loop length should not exceed 2 inches in total length.

Step 2   Wind your thread back to the rear of the shank and tie in a 2-inch piece of Hareline's Shrimp Pink Krystal flash Chenille. Wind the chenille until it covers the rear section of the shank where the two wires meet and come together. Secure the chenille with several thread wraps and cut off the excess. Take and cut off a 3-inch section of Enrico Puglisi 1.5 Short Purple Foxy brush and attach to the shank in front of the chenille. Wet your fingers with some water and primp the fibers back. Palmer the brush forward with three or four wraps and secure. Cut off the remaining material and make sure the wire is pushed down flat.

Step 3   Take 20 strands of Pink Lateral Scale flash roughly 6 inches long and tie them in on one side and then fold over the excess to the other side. Make sure to tie this group of Flash covers all open areas to create total coverage 365 degrees around the shank.

Step 4   Palmer a nice rear collar with a lavender guinea feather, by tying the feather in by the tip so that the curve of the feather is facing down over top of the fly. This should look like an upside-down boat. Slowly wind the guinea toward the eye while pulling back on the feather fibers so they don't become tangled in each wrap. I typically wrap around the shank four times and tie off, but you can go thicker by adding a couple extra wraps. If you would like a thinner profile you can also strip one side of the guinea and the tie it in following the same steps.

Step 5   Attach a 3-inch piece of Flat Diamond Braid in front of the guinea collar and secure. Evenly wrap the flat diamond braid toward the eye of the shank stopping where the two wires are bent and meet to form the eye. When tying on the longer shanks and building a longer body I do like to put a thin coat of Crazy Glue over the body to prevent unwinding or damage from fish teeth.

Step 6   Attach a set of four rainbow Senyodelic bead chain eyes to the bottom off the shank where the front two wires meet to form the shank eye and secure with several figure eight thread wraps. You can add a drop of super glue to the middle of the eyes for added strength. Cut off another 3-inch piece of the Shrimp Pink Krystal flash chenille and make a figure eight wrap around the bead chain eyes. Take another 3-inch piece of Enrico Puglisi's Purple 1.5 short Foxy brush and tie in front the Senyodelic bead chain. Palmer several wraps in front of the eyes to form a solid underwing.

Step 7   Take 20 strands of Pink Lateral Scale Flash roughly 6 inches long and tie them in on one side and then fold over the excess to the other side. Rotate the fly and repeat the same process with twenty strands of Grape Flashabou, just make sure to tie this group of Flashabou in on the open areas to create total coverage 365 degrees around the shank. Next take three strands of 4-inch long Blue Smolt Wacko Hackle and lay them in along each side of the fly to create a lateral line.

Step 8   Palmer a nice collar with Natural Guinea feather, by tying the feather in by the tip so that the curve of the feather is facing down over top of the fly. This should look like an upside-down boat. Slowly wind the guinea toward the eye while pulling back on the feather fibers so they don't become tangled in each wrap. I typically wrap around the shank four times and tie off, but you can go thicker by adding a couple extra wraps. If you would like a thinner profile you can also strip one side of the guinea and the tie it in following the same steps. You can add a set of Jungle Cock Eyes, or a set of Hareline's Real Fake Jungle Cock. This is optional and is not required to finish off the pattern, but is preferred. I have found that fishing patterns with a very visible eye can be a trigger on predatory fish such as steelhead, salmon, and trout.

7

FUSION DUB SCULPIN

Goby, Sculpin, Mad Tom, Chub, and Baby Sucker are just a few baitfish that I've come across over the years. It really doesn't matter what fishery I'm on, it is certain one of these species can be found. Sculpin patterns have become a staple in places like the Great Lakes, Western trout rivers, Alaska, and just about every notable trout stream across the country.

Over the past decade the Great Lakes saw an explosion of exotic species dumped into our ecosystems. Where many worried about the invasion, our Great Lakes predatory fish took advantage of the new-found food sources and packed on the pounds. When the round goby was introduced to the Great Lakes by cargo ships dumping ballast water, many believed we were in danger of losing a lot of our gamefish. This was due in part to the round goby actively attacking the nesting sites and redds of spawning game fish.

It wasn't long before I caught and inspected a round goby. I was fishing the mouth of Elk Creek, a Pennsylvania tributary that runs into Lake Erie. Gobies look very similar to the sculpin I have seen in the spring creeks, but with brilliant purple and pearlescent green hues. One evening as I was coming back to the boat launch and access area to leave, I couldn't ignore the amount of splashing and activity along the rock walls built to stop erosion along the of the bank and ramp. I walked over and watched for the next hour, several small schools of lake-run brown trout and steelhead were ambushing and attacking goby off the structure. I will never forget that experience and what I saw that evening.

Most of the sculpin imitations I fished at the time consisted of either wool or deer hair for the head, and a long piece of zonker rabbit strip for the body and tail. The problem was the rabbit took forever to finally get soaked enough to sink. When the rabbit finally did become saturated it was heavy, especially when coupled with a wool head, and a pain in the butt to cast. I decided to incorporate a more synthetic approach, which would also imitate the pearlescent and purple hues much better than naturals. Also I could keep the fly light regardless of length due to the synthetic's ability to shed water quickly.

The design is all about holding a big head with skinny body profile. The marabou tail and collar give just the right amount of natural motion without imparting any action to the fly. The synthetics such as Aqua Veil provide the contrast, color hues, sliminess and mottling effect to match the hatch. The stacked fusion dub head allows you to mix colors effectively and still hold and retain a fat head profile underwater. I fish this pattern around any type of underwater structure. Most of the time just swinging the fly into and around structure does the job, but at times I do like to impart extra movement by twitching the rod tip, or with short line strips followed by an extended pause.

Target Species   Migratory and resident trout, Alaskan rainbow, grayling, char, Great Lakes steelhead, and smallmouth bass

Favorite Color Combos   Olive/Brown, Olive/Black, Black/Purple, and Tan/Brown. All with Copper, Gold, Silver, and UV Pearl flash hues.

FUSION DUB SCULPIN MATERIALS

Shank   40mm Black Flymen Fishing Company Senyo Steelhead/Salmon Shank (40SA-11)

Thread   UTC 140 or Veevus 6/0 (V6-11)

Wire   Hareline Dubbin Inc. Senyo's Intruder Wire or Berkley Original Fused Fireline (THW-11)

Tail   Hareline Dubbin Inc. Olive Marabou Blood Quill (MSBQ-263)

Flash   Speckled Flashabou Copper (FLA-6934)

Body   Senyo's Pepperoni Aqua Veil (SA8)

Collar 1   Hareline Dubbin Inc. Fiery Brown Schlappen (SCHL-114)

Collar 2   Hareline Dubbin Inc. Rusty Brown Guinea Feather (SGF-323)

Flash   Pearl Lateral Scale (LSC-1703)

Head 1   Senyo's Tobacco Fusion Dub (FUS14)

Head 2   Senyo's Midnight Fusion Dub (FUS8)

Head 3   Senyo's Emerald Fusion Dub (FUS4)

Hook   Partridge, Daiichi, Owner, Gamakatsu size 2–4 Intruder Style (D2557)

FUSION DUB SCULPIN TYING INSTRUCTIONS

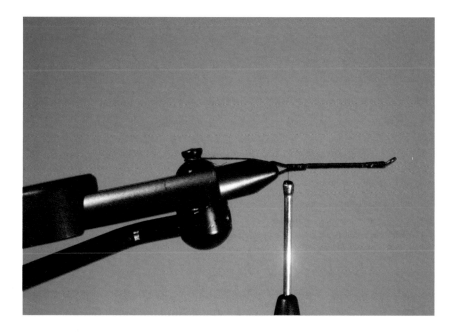

Step 1   Place a 40mm Senyo Steelhead Shank from Flymen Fishing Company in your vise. Attach your UTC 140 or Veevus 6/0 thread and evenly coat the entire shank and close both front and rear loops with a thin base of thread. Cut off a 4-inch piece of Senyo's Intruder Wire or 30-pound Berkley Fireline and secure it to both sides of the shank with several thread wraps. Take the tag ends through the bottom of the front loop and fold over the top of the shank. Pull tight over the top of the shank and tie down securely with several even thread wraps. Adding glue for strength is optional. Your wire loop length should not exceed 2 inches in total length.

Step 2   Wind your thread back to the rear of the shank and tie in a full marabou plume equal to the length of the shank. I like to hold the marabou to allow the plumes to distribute evenly around the shank as you apply thread wraps to lock the feather down. You can simply twist the feather around the shank with your fingers as well. When I use marabou as a tail on this fly, I prefer to leave the stem in the marabou of this pattern. This adds extra stiffness to the tail without hindering the natural movement, and also keeps the material from wanting to tangle on my wire or hook. Add three to six strands of Speckled Copper Flashabou to each side of the marabou tail.

Step 3   Tie in a 3-inch piece of Pepperoni Aqua Veil and make several wraps evenly coating the shank as you move forward. You should stop roughly ⅛ inch away from where the front two wires of the shank come together to form the eye of the shank. Cut off any remaining aqua veil and secure with several thread wraps.

Step 4   Palmer a nice collar with Schlappen feather, by tying the feather in by the tip so that the curve of the feather is facing down over top of the fly. This should look like an upside-down boat. Slowly wind the Schlappen toward the eye while pulling back on the feather fibers so they don't become tangled in each wrap. I typically wrap around the shank four times and tie off, but you can go thicker by adding a couple extra wraps. If you would like a thinner profile you can also strip one side of the feather and tie it in following the same steps. Tie in three to six strands of Pearl Lateral Scale over top of the Schlappen and secure.

Step 5   Palmer a nice collar with Fiery Brown Natural Guinea feather, by tying the feather in by the tip so that the curve of the feather is facing down over top of the fly. This should look like an upside-down boat. Slowly wind the guinea toward the eye while pulling back on the feather fibers so they don't become tangled in each wrap. I typically wrap around the shank four times and tie off, but you can go thicker by adding a couple extra wraps. If you would like a thinner profile you can also strip one side of the guinea and tie it in following the same steps. Take a clump of Tobacco Fusion Dubbing and center tie it in with several thread wraps. Fold the dubbing over itself and bring the thread to the front of the dubbing. Some combing may be required to force the material to flow toward the rear and to free material tips and fibers from being caught in the thread wraps.

Step 6   Take a clump of Midnight Fusion Dubbing and center tie it in with several thread wraps. Fold the dubbing over itself and bring the thread to the front of the dubbing. Some combing may be required to force the material to flow toward the rear and to free material tips and fibers from being caught in the thread wraps.

Step 7   Take a clump of Emerald Fusion Dubbing and center tie it in with several thread wraps. Fold the dubbing over itself and bring the thread to the front of the dubbing.

Step 8   Some extra and rough combing may be required to blend the three dubbing colors together and free any further loose fibers. Finish the fly off with a good thread head, and a rough scissor trim of the fusion dubbing.

8

EGG RAIDER

A client and I were having lunch on a high bluff overlooking a local steelhead tributary. It was the peak of the spring steelhead season on the Great Lakes. The conditions had taken a turn for the worse over the week and the rivers started to become dangerously low and extremely clear. My client was working hard but missed out on the few good opportunities provided by some post-spawn or "drop back" steelhead.

I remained in high spirits knowing we still had half the day on the river remaining, and still plenty of fish to go around. Getting ready to move, we heard what sounded like rocks falling off the bluff and crashing into the river. We watched as a pod of bachelor steelhead just started going crazy.

About 50 feet upriver of the pod, we noticed a solo hen and her mate spawning. There were roughly five of them all around the 24–28 inch class.

A few minutes passed by when all the sudden the big courting male and the bucks began attacking something and trashing the water below. They were fired up and moving fast. I was pretty excited at what I was seeing. It finally came together as I watched a smaller fish go belly up and beach itself just a little downstream. As fast as I could get myself down the bluff I found this small 4–5 inch creek chub nearly torn in half. It was only a minute later when the water erupted again for a third time.

I made it back to the top of the bluff and looked to see where these creek chub were hiding. I couldn't believe it! They were all in single file against the opposite shale wall, slowly swimming forward until they were in line with the spawning hen. Then they would peel off and attack the bed for its eggs, at least fifty creek chubs were willing to risk it all, and the steelhead weren't going to let it happen without a fight. Now that we knew what was going on, we switched to light tips and longer leaders and I opened my box to a few Egg Raiders in olive/copper/gold. I just tied these for fun the week before and this was the perfect situation to fish them.

We timed it perfectly and dropped a good cast as the water was starting to churn. The fly came across the bachelor pod perfectly and was completely ripped off the leader on a full-out cartwheel down the river. Excited, I threw another Egg Raider to my client and waited for the show to start again. On his next cast the fly received an epic grab, and a fat 25-inch buck would eventually come to hand. Over the next several years my client has caught bigger steelhead, but we always come back to talking about this incredible two hours on the river and the creek chub experience neither of us has ever seen again. Today I fish this pattern in a multitude of color schemes and fisheries where any fish species is spawning. The Great Lakes and Alaska are the two most notable places where this fly produces best.

Target Species   Migratory brown trout, Alaskan char, Great Lakes steelhead, and Great Lakes salmon species.

Favorite Color Combos   Olive/Brown/Copper, Olive/Copper/Gold, Black/Purple/Blue, and White/Olive/Pearl

EGG RAIDER MATERIALS

Shank   Inexpensive 3x long straight eye streamer hook cut off at the bend

Bead   8mm Orange/Pink Super Eggs (SEL-14)

Thread   Purple UTC 140 or Veevus 6/0 (V6-11)

Wire   Hareline Dubbin Inc. Senyo Intruder Wire or Berkley Original Fused Fireline (THW-289)

Tail   Hareline Dubbin Inc. Purple over Fuchsia Micro Pulsator Strips (MPS-18)

Flash   Rainbow Flashabou (FLA-6924)

Rear Collar   Hareline Dubbin Inc. Hot Pink Marabou Blood Quill (MSBQ-188)

Body   Senyo's Raspberry Aqua Veil (SA-11)

Collar   Hareline Dubbin Inc. Purple Marabou Blood Quill (MSBQ-298)

Head   Senyo's Purple Shaggy Dub (SSD-298)

Eyes   Senyodelic Bead Chain (SBCM-306) or Hareline Dubbin Inc. Plastic Beady Eyes (PBE)

Hook   Partridge, Gamakatsu, Daiichi, or Owner size 2–4 intruder style hook.

EGG RAIDER TYING INSTRUCTIONS

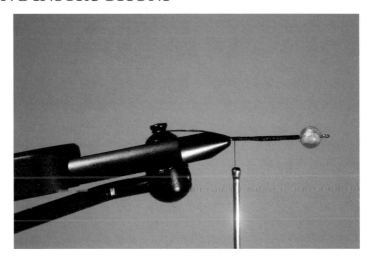

Step 1   Take a 3x-long straight eye streamer hook that has been cut off at the bend, and slide on an 8mm Super egg bead before clamping it in your vise. Attach your UTC 140 or Veevus 6/0 thread and evenly coat the entire hook from the bead to the back with a thin base of thread. Cut off a 4-inch piece of Senyo's Intruder Wire or 30-pound Berkley Fireline and secure it to both sides of the shank with several thread wraps. Take the tag ends and fold over the top of the hook and tie down. Adding glue for strength is a good idea with this pattern. Your wire loop length should not exceed 2 inches in total length.

Step 2   Wind your thread back to the rear of the shank and tie in a 4-inch piece of the purple-over-pink Pulsator strip. I like using the Pulsator strips for this pattern versus the standard ⅛ rabbit strips, because the hide is very thin and it takes this version a lot less time to absorb water and start to swim well.

Step 3   Tie in your Hot Pink Marabou plume over the bunny strip. I double-check each marabou feather and pull out the top portion of the stem to allow the feather to breathe easier and obtain more movement from the water current. Tie in six to eight strands of rainbow Flashabou over the top of the marabou and Pulsator rabbit strip tail.

Step 4   Tie in a 3-inch piece of Senyo's Raspberry Aqua Veil chenille and palmer the chenille forward to create the body of the pattern. This material is very easy to work with, when you wet and stroke the chenille fibers all in the same direction toward the rear of the fly. This method will ensure that as you wind forward, all the fibers will flow and negate excess bulk by over wrapping the material.

Step 5   Tie in a second Purple Marabou plume over the Raspberry Aqua Veil, and again double check the marabou feather and pull out the top portion of the stem. Tie in additional six to eight strands of rainbow Flashabou over the top of the purple marabou.

Step 6   Take a generous clump of Purple Shaggy Dub and trim both ends of the clump to make the material even on both sides. You may need to use your scissors and cut open any extra loops of material as well. Spread the shaggy dub evenly on the side you plan on having it tied. By doing this, it should expose the center of the material and allow you to push the shaggy dub over the egg and onto the hook. Secure it in the center with several thread wraps. After this step, fold over the other half of the shaggy dub and bring your thread to the front. Firmly hold and stroke back the material and add a drop of super glue to the base of the shaggy dub. Both Loon Flow and Clear Cure Goo Hydro products will work in the same manner as super glue.

Step 7   Attach a section of four Senyodelic Bead Chain Eyes to the bottom of the hook just behind the egg bead and secure with several figure-8 wraps and a drop of glue or epoxy. Do not try to over trim the Shaggy dub after the fly is complete; let the fibers kind of flow as they please. This adds another element of movement and this material is very prone to tangle in fish teeth.

9

ICE MAN MINNOW

Have you ever found yourself staring at that single tree branch hanging over the river? You know the one that has more indicators, flies, and tippet attached to it than what your local fly shop has in stock. How many times have you watched your buddy looking up at your favorite fly that he's lodged 10 feet into the tree either behind or into the tree across the river? I have a fun little tradition for exactly these types of occasions. It's simple, I just turn around and face the woods, and pray to the gods that I will provide another fly.

I can honestly say that the Ice Man Minnow is pretty much the only fast tie fly pattern I have in my arsenal. The cool thing about this pattern is that by using tubing, you can tie five or six flies on the vise at the same time. I first tied this fly when it became apparent that after guiding all week long I really didn't have much time in between trips to stock my boxes. I also needed a pattern that I could use for all the drought and clear water conditions that we encounter all season long.

I also wanted a small fly that I could swing as a tandem rig, drop under an indicator, and cast from the beaches. This simple fly provides a schooling baitfish, hatching fry, or stunned bait appeal. I needed function and purpose with the imitation matching the natural in appearance only. The Ice Man Minnow becomes completely translucent but still retains its tear-drop profile. If you want action out of this fly, you need to impart it yourself because you will get no help from the material here.

Target Species   Migratory and resident trout, Alaskan char and lake trout, Great Lakes steelhead/Atlantic salmon, Great Lakes salmon, and lake-run pike.

Favorite Color Combos   Blue/Pink/Pearl, Olive/Chartreuse/Pearl, Gray/Orange/Pearl, and Tan/Shrimp/Pearl

ICE MAN MINNOW MATERIALS

Thread   Veevus Red 6/0 (6V-310)

Tube   Small or Medium Poly tubing Clear (SMP-65)

Belly   Senyo's Laser Dub (SL)

Underwing   Hareline Dubbin Inc. Ice Dubbing (ICE)

Head   Senyo's Fusion Dubbing (FUS)

Eyes   ⅛ 3D Holographic Eyes Silver (83D)

Epoxy   Clear Cure Goo Brushable (CG-7) or Loon UV Fly Finish Thin (LN-91)

Hook   Partridge, Daiichi, Tube Hook size 8–10 (D1640)

Note   Tube fly tying starter kit or pin is required for this fly. The pattern can be tied individually on the hook as well.

ICE MAN MINNOW TYING INSTRUCTIONS

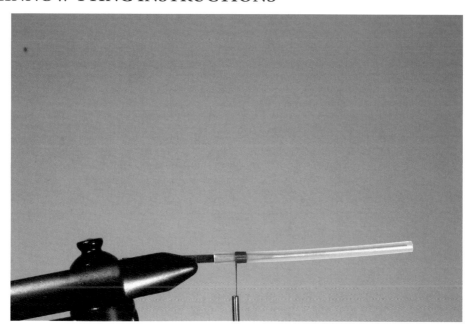

Step 1   Take a 5-inch long piece of small or medium clear plastic tubing and slide it onto your tying pin or needle. Start roughly a ¼-inch from the rear of the tubing and attach 6/0 red tying thread. The red of the thread will actually double as a gill or hot spot for the fly. Lay an even thread base over the tube to allow the material to hold secure without slipping around the tube.

Step 2   Take a sparse pinch of Laser dubbing and pull the fibers apart until you get all the dubbing fibers flowing in the same direction. Tie the laser dubbing in at the center of the clump with several thread wraps. The remaining laser dubbing is then folded over onto itself. End with your thread brought to the front.

Step 3 Next, grab and separate a small clump of ice dubbing to get all the fibers flowing in the same direction. Instead of tying the dubbing by the center, stagger the wing and tie the ice dubbing in with ¾ of the ice dub fibers off the rear and a ¼ of the ice dub to be folded over itself in the front. Make sure you secure the ice dubbing down with at least three or four tight wraps of thread before moving in front of the ice dubbing. It is not uncommon to lose a few fibers that were too long or didn't get fully secured due to material length.

Step 4 To finish off his section of the body of the fly, grab another sparse pinch of laser dubbing and pull the fibers apart until you get all the dubbing fibers flowing in the same direction. From here, tie in the laser dubbing at the center of the clump with several thread wraps.

Step 5 The remaining laser dubbing is then folded over onto itself and your thread brought to the front. At this point you can either whip finish or apply a little glue and cut the thread. Start the process again by repeating the previous steps.

Step 6 As above.

Step 7   As above.

Step 8   Add a set of silver ⅛ inch 3D prismatic eye to each side of the laser dub head. The eye should be positioned where the top of the eye rests on the laser dubbing, and the bottom of the eye rests on the red thread base on fly tubing.

Step 9   Turn the fly over and coat the thread and eyes with Clear Cure Goo or Loon Fly Finish.

Step 10   Use a UV lamp or light to cure epoxy.

Step 11 At this point, you can decide how many you would like to make and how many colors you will need. Simply move forward a ¼-inch on the tubing and apply another thread base. Repeat the tying steps above until you have created five or six minnows on a single piece of tubing. From this point I put the entire stick in my box and just cut one off the tube as I need them. By using both Copic and Sharpie permanent markers, I can easily dress up the laser and ice dubbing to match a wide variety of baitfish. I not only have markers available on my tying bench, but I also carry a small selection with me on the river to make quick changes to my fly patterns.

10

Storm Trooper AKA "Alaskan Leech"

I'm standing in the waters of an amazing Alaskan char fishery called the Ugashik Narrows. The water is teaming with Sockeye and the char are focused on the eggs being flushed into the lower lake. I'm fishing with a few friends and it it's not long before we're scoring silvery blue chrome char on variety of painted beads. We decide to switch up tactics and offer a few tasty steamers into the outlet of the lower lake. Our guide had told us stories of 30-plus inch char and a shot at a few lake trout prowling along the dropoff. At that time I had never taken a lake trout on the fly, so I was pretty excited to have this opportunity.

After dinner the evening before our fly out, a bunch of us were sitting around the table and tying various patterns incorporating different beads, components, and the Fish Skulls from Flymen Fishing Company. The infusion of an array of synthetic materials and tying components really allow you to have fun and be creative with your patterns. Add beer, whiskey, tobacco, and fun people to the mix and it really allows for you to free your mind.

When you go to Alaska in late August and September it's hard sometimes not to get caught up in the bead bite. Millions of eggs are flushing downstream and hungry rainbow trout and Dolly Varden are packing on some serious pounds to get ready for the long winter. I can be honest and say that after experiencing this a couple times, I literally became bored. Let's make no mistake here and cast away any doubt about the use of beads, as they are efficient and extremely effective fish catchers. It came down to how I can incorporate the bead bite into my favorite method of fishing. Personally I enjoy every opportunity to swing a fly. I like being busy and casting all day, and I enjoy the pull or take from a fish on a streamer over everything else.

Target Species   Migratory trout, Alaskan char and lake trout, Great Lakes steelhead, Great Lakes salmon species.

Favorite Color Combos   Orange/Pink/Copper, Olive/Chartreuse/Gold, Black/Purple/Blue, and White/Olive/Pearl.

STORM TROOPER MATERIALS

Shank   Flymen Fishing Company Black 40mm Senyo Steelhead and Salmon Shank (40SA-11)

Thread   UTC 70 or Veevus 10/0 (V10-11)

Wire   Hareline Dubbin Inc. Senyo Intruder Wire or Berkley Original Fused Fireline (THW-11)

Beads   Two 8mm orange or pink Super Eggs (SEL-14)

Bead Wire   30-pound Berkley Fire Line or 15-pound fluorocarbon

Under Body   EP Senyo's 1.5 Chrome Black Chromatic Brush (SCB-2)

Legs   Hareline Dubbin Inc. Black/Red Fleck Crazy Legs (CL-15)

Wing   Hareline Dubbin Inc. Black Rabbit Zonker Strip (RS-6)

Flash   Gun Metal Flashabou (FLA-6916)

Head 1   Senyo's Midnight Fusion Dubbing (FUS8)

Head 2   Flymen Fishing Company Fish Skull Fish Mask #5 (FFM-5)

Eyes   Flymen Fishing Company Small Earth Living Eyes (4LE-1)

Epoxy   Clear Cure Goo (CG-7) or Loon Outdoors UV Clear Fly Finish thin (LN91)

Hook   Partridge, Gamakatsu, or Owner size 2–4 intruder style hook (D2557)

STORM TROOPER TYING INSTRUCTIONS

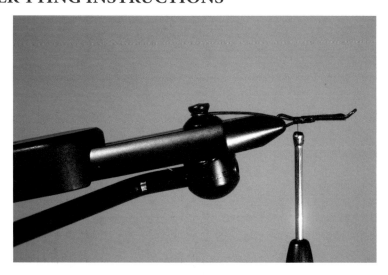

Step 1   Place a 40mm Senyo Steelhead Shank from Flymen Fishing Company in your vise. Attach your UTC 70 or Veevus 10/0 thread and evenly coat the entire shank and close both front and rear loops with a thin base of thread. Cut off a 4-inch piece of Senyo's Intruder Wire or 30-pound Berkley Fireline and secure it to both sides of the shank with several thread wraps. Take the tag ends through the bottom of the front loop and fold over the top of the shank. Pull tight over the top of the shank and tie down securely with several even thread wraps. Adding glue for strength is optional. Your wire loop length should not exceed 2 inches in total length.

Step 2   Wind your thread to the rear of the shank and rotate the vise 180 degrees to the bottom of the shank. Tie in a 4-inch piece of Berkley Fire line by one end and allow the other end to simply stick out the rear of the shank. At this time, you should rotate your vise back to the upright position. Tie in a 3-inch section of Chrome Black 1.5 Chromatic Brush and make four or five wraps forward to form a compact and tight ball of material. An easy way to get the foxy brush to fold back and the fibers to flow the same direction, is to get them wet and pull back tight on the fibers while you are winding forward. Take a needle or a wire brush and pick or comb out the material so it flows nicely to the rear of the shank.

Step 3 Grab a set of Black/Red Flecked Crazy Legs and center tie them to each side of the brush. The easiest way to attach rubber legs to your pattern is to take the legs behind your tying thread, wrap them around, and lift them up toward the tie in point. This will use the tension from the bobbin to hold the rubber legs in place making it very easy to secure them.

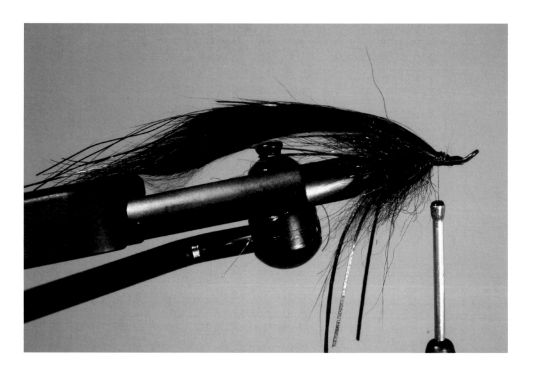

Step 4 Tie in a 4-inch piece of Hareline Dubbin Inc. Black 1/8 Zonker Strip and secure in over the top of the fox and allow to hang off the rear of the shank. Attach eight to ten strands of Gun Metal Flashabou over the rabbit Zonker strip and secure with several thread wraps.

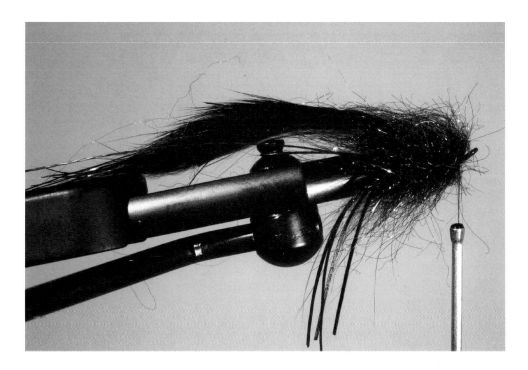

Step 5   Take a clump of Midnight Fusion Dubbing and center tie the dubbing around the shank. Fold over the fusion dubbing onto itself and brush out toward the rear.

Step 6   Rotate your vise back to the bottom and grab the piece of Fireline we left hanging off the back. Take and slide onto the two Fireline 8mm orange/pink Super Egg beads. Now we want the beads to sit in the belly of the fly, but not to be so tight they won't move. So pull the Fireline toward the front of the fly and secure it, but check that the beads still have a little movement. Once the beads are secured, rotate the vise back to the top.

Step 7   Apply a liberal thread base and a bit of Loon Fly Finish to the inside of a #5 Flymen fishing Company Fish Skull Fish Mask. Push it onto the shank and snuggly against the shaggy dubbing. Cut your thread and bring it to the front of the skull and re-attach. Make a small thread head to keep the skull from moving. The Flymen Fish Skull Fish Masks come with eyes included, but I prefer the Flymen Earth Living eyes. They are much more predominant and vibrant. Place a Living eye in each socket of the Fish Skull. To finish the fly I apply a thin coating of brushable Clear Cure Goo or Loon Fly Finish over the eyes and thread head. Simply hit with a UV light for a few seconds, and cut the thread.

11

DR. FEEL GOOD

If you can't tell already, I listen to a lot of music while I am tying. Some artists just have that energy to help you push through an evening on the vise. I almost compare it to pumping yourself up for a workout at the gym. Most of the time I'm so jazzed for the next day's fishing excursion I can't sleep. Instead I stay awake most of the night tying flies for the next day. Typically, it's needless overkill because I already have too many flies stuffed in boxes and baggies.

The Dr. Feel Good is my favorite leech pattern, and a great tying alternative to using rabbit Zonker and crosscut strips. You will notice throughout this book that I prefer not to use rabbit in most of my flies. I realize that rabbit has a ton of lifelike action, but it has its downsides too. I hate fishing rabbit fur in winter because it turns into a brick of ice from the frigid air. I hate that it takes forever to saturate, and when it is fully saturated, it becomes heavy. When it dries out after fishing it becomes stiff as a board. Most of all, I dislike the fact I can never get the same amount, length, and consistency of fur on every strip. Sure it's natural and comes the way it is, but during commercial tying, it becomes a pain in the butt searching for the perfect material.

Target Species   Migratory brown trout, Alaskan char, Great Lakes and PNW steelhead, Pacific and Great Lakes salmon species, and pike

Favorite Color Combos   Orange/Pink/Copper, Olive/Chartreuse/Gold, Black/Purple/Blue, and White/Olive/Pearl

DR. FEEL GOOD MATERIALS

Shank   Flymen Fishing Company Copper 25mm Senyo Steelhead/Salmon Shank (25SA-271)

Thread   UTC 70 or Veevus 10/0 FL. Orange (10V-137)

Wire   Hareline Dubbin Inc. Senyo Intruder Wire or Berkley Original Fused Fireline (THW-271)

Rear Underbody   Enrico Puglisi Hot Orange 1.5 Short Foxy Brush (FXS-187)

Wing   Hareline Dubbin Inc. Shell Pink and Hot Pink Shimmer Fringe (IDM-10) and Copper Mirage Flashabou (FLA-3306)

Body   EP Senyo 3.0 Flame Chromatic Brush (WSC-7)

Collar   Hareline Dubbin Inc. Orange Strung Guinea feather (SGF-271)

Eyes   Hareline Dubbin Inc. Real Fake Jungle Cock (FJ-5)

Hook   Partridge, Gamakatsu, or Owner size 2–4 Intruder style hook (D2557)

DR. FEEL GOOD TYING INSTRUCTIONS

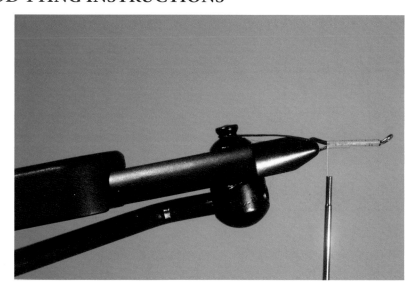

Step 1 Place a copper 25mm Senyo Steelhead Shank from Flymen Fishing Company in your vise. Attach your UTC 70 or Veevus 10/0 thread and evenly coat the entire shank and close both front and rear loops with a thin base of thread. Cut off a 4-inch piece of Senyo's Intruder Wire or 30-pound Berkley Fireline and secure it to both sides of the shank with several thread wraps. Take the tag ends through the bottom of the front loop and fold over the top of the shank. Pull tight over the top of the shank and tie down securely with several even thread wraps. Adding glue for strength is optional. Your wire loop length should not exceed 2 inches in total length.

Step 2 Tie in a 3-inch piece of Hot Orange EP 1½-inch foxy brush and make four or five wraps forward to form a compact, tight ball of material. An easy way to get the foxy brush to fold back and fibers to flow the same direction is to get them wet and pull back tight on the fibers while you are winding forward. Take a needle or a wire brush and pick or comb out the material so it flows nicely to the rear of the shank.

Step 3   Tie in roughly a ¼-inch section of Hareline's Shell Pink/Hot Pink Shimmer Fringe over the top of the fox. Next grab roughly twenty strands of copper/opal Mirage Flashabou and apply over the top of the Shimmer Fringe. Try to stagger or keep the Flashabou uneven as you tie them in. It is important to note that I try at all cost to keep the ends of the Flashabou uneven to give it a tapered versus uniformed or straight edged look.

Step 4   Take a 4-inch long piece of Flame EP Senyo 3.0 inch Chromatic Brush. Trim off the bottom roughly ⅛ of the fur, and bend the wire to form a reverse "L" and tie in the wire with several thread wraps. Evenly and without wrapping over top of the material, palmer toward the front of the shank. Make sure to leave about ⅛-inch of the shank clean for the next step.

Step 5   Palmer a nice collar with an Orange Guinea feather, by tying the feather in by the tip so that the curve of the feather is facing down over top of the fly. This should look like an upside-down boat. Slowly wind the guinea toward the eye while pulling back on the feather fibers so they don't become tangled in each wrap. I typically wrap around the shank four times and tie off, but you can go thicker by adding a couple of extra wraps. If you would like a thinner profile you can also strip one side of the guinea and tie it in following the same steps.

Step 6   You can add a set of Jungle Cock Eyes, or a set of Hareline's Real Fake Jungle Cock. This is optional and is not required to finish off the pattern, but is preferred. I have found that fishing patterns with a very visible eye can be a trigger on predatory fish such as steelhead, salmon, and trout. *Note:* If you chose to add your eyes make sure to build a small and uniform head of thread, and coat with a slight about of Crazy Glue. Crazy Glue is now available with a brush allowing clean and easy application. I rarely whip finish or half hitch anymore. The glue is stronger than any knot you can tie.

12

GenX Muddler

The Muddler Minnow was one of the first flies I have ever fished. As a kid just figuring out fly fishing, the muddler minnow was a staple pattern in the fly shop bins, which would catch everything from trout, panfish, and smallmouth bass on my local streams and ponds. In the later years I began tying the muddler much larger to target both steelhead and salmon. Today I still fish Don Gapen's famous pattern, just with a little more synthetic adaptation with a modern twist to an American classic!

I've heard it said many times over the years that synthetic materials are ruining the traditions of fly tying and the history and foundations laid down over the years. I firmly believe that tradition in fly tying is alive and well, and that by adapting to the new age materials and fishing these flies that we are paying homage and keeping their inspirations, creations, and spirit alive for generations to come.

Target Species   Migratory and resident trout, Alaskan char, PNW and Great Lakes steelhead, Great lakes Atlantic salmon, Pacific salmon and smallmouth bass.

Favorite Color Combos   Olive/yellow, brown/copper, black/purple, black/blue, tan/white, black/red

GENX MUDDLER MATERIALS

Shank   Flymen Fishing Company 40mm Senyo Steelhead/Salmon Shank (40SA-23)

Thread   UTC 140 (U140-11) or Veevus 6/0 (6V-11)

Wire   Hareline Dubbin Inc. Senyo Intruder Wire or Berkley Original Fused Fireline (THW-298)

Tail   Hareline Dubbin Inc. Purple Lady Amherst Tail Center Feather (LAC-298)

Body   Lagartun Purple Mini Flat Braid or Hareline Dubbin Inc. Purple Flat Diamond Braid (FD-298)

Rib   Veevus French Silver Tinsel (VTM-344)

Under Body   EP Senyo midnight 1.5 Chromatic Brush (SCB-11)

Wing   Hareline Dubbin Inc. Purple Arctic Fox Tail Hair (AFT-298)

Flash   Pearl Lateral Scale (LSC-1703)

Collar   Purple Silver Pheasant feather (SPF-298) and Senyo's Electric Grape Fusion Dub (FUS-3)

Eyes   Jungle Cock or Hareline Dubbin Inc. Real Fake Jungle Cock (FJ-5)

Head   Hareline Dubbin Inc. Black Dyed Deer Body Hair (DD-11)

Hook   Partridge, Gamakatsu, or Owner size 2 stinger or Intruder style hook (D2557)

GENX MUDDLER TYING INSTRUCTIONS

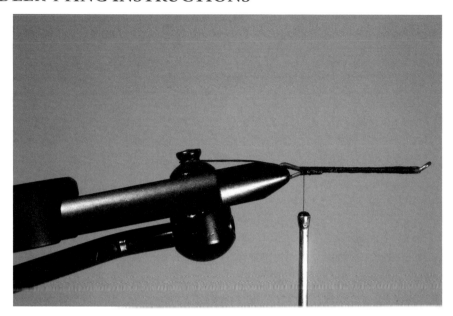

Step 1   Place a Blue 40mm Senyo Steelhead Shank from Flymen Fishing Company in your vise. Attach your UTC 140 or Veevus 6/0 thread and evenly coat the entire shank and close both front and rear loops with a thin base of thread. Cut off a 4-inch piece of Senyo's Intruder Wire or 30-pound Berkley Fireline and secure it to both sides of the shank with several thread wraps. Take the tag ends through the bottom of the front loop and fold over the top of the shank. Pull tight over the top of the shank and tie down securely with several even thread wraps. Adding glue for strength is optional. Your wire loop length should not exceed 2 inches in total length.

Step 2   Tie in a section of Purple Lady Amherst Tail feather that is roughly 2 inches long and secure all fibers on top of the shank with several thread wraps.

Step 3   Tie in a 3-inch piece of Purple Flat Diamond Braid and a 3-inch piece of Veevus Silver French oval tinsel. Evenly wrap the mini flat braid toward the eye of the shank stopping where the two wires are bent and meet to form the eye. Take the oval French tinsel and make five or six evenly-spaced wraps forward to the same point where the two wires meet and secure with several thread wraps. When tying on the longer shanks and building a longer body I like to put a thin coat of Crazy Glue over the body to prevent unwinding or damage from fish teeth.

Step 4   Take a 4-inch piece of an EP Senyo 1.5 inch midnight Chromatic brush and tie it in by the wire. To make it easy, wet your fingers and stroke all the fibers of the Chromic Brush toward the rear of the fly. After four or five wraps you should secure with several thread wraps and trim away any excess materials. Take a wire brush or a needle and lightly comb out and pick out any stuck materials.

Step 5   Take a clump of Hareline's Purple Arctic Fox Fur that is roughly 3–4 inches long, and tie in centered and over the top of the pattern. It's ok to pull out some of the thick short under fur, but do not remove the guard hairs from the fur during this step. Take three individual strands of Lateral Scale and center tie them in on the top of the wing. Fold over the flash and secure with several thread wraps. Try to keep all the lengths of the flash uneven. This is so the flash will taper and reflect at different lengths and doesn't come to a straight line.

Step 6   Take a small clump of Senyo's Electric Grape Fusion Dubbing and center tie the clump in front of the fox wing. Fold over to rear the remaining fusion dubbing and bring your thread back to the front.

Step 7   Palmer a nice collar with a purple Silver Pheasant Tail feather, by tying the feather in by the tip so that the curve of the feather is facing down over top of the fly. This should look like an upside-down boat. Slowly wind the pheasant toward the eye while pulling back on the feather fibers so they don't become tangled in each wrap. I typically wrap around the shank four times and tie off, but you can go thicker by adding a couple extra wraps. If you would like a thinner profile you can also strip one side of the pheasant and tie it in following the same steps.

Step 8   Add a large set of Jungle Cock Eyes, or a set of Hareline's Real Fake Jungle Cock. This is optional and is not required to finish off the pattern, but is preferred. I have found that fishing patterns with a very visible eye can be a trigger on predatory fish such as steelhead, salmon, trout, and bass. Cut out roughly a ½-inch section of the black dyed deer hair. I don't typically stack my hair, but if you do, this would be the time to do it. I prefer the uneven rugged look for the finished product, similar to the original Muddler Minnow. Tie in your hair and spin it around the shank and secure with several thread wraps. Realize that you may, or may not need to do this step twice. That is dependent on how much room on your shank and how much deer hair you use.

Step 9   I prefer to scissor trim and maintain a rough appearance. Also, the bigger head allows for more water to be pushed around the fly. The end result is more movement to the materials behind the head. I also add a light coating of Crazy Glue to the front of the deer hair. This is an easy application with a brush. This adds durability to the pattern, but is optional and more or less a tier's choice.

13

THE SHAGGY DUDE

Every so often my oldest son Bryce comes down to the tying room. I try very hard not to push him in any direction, more or less out of fear he may not want to fly fish or tie flies. I really want him to find his own way and come to appreciate this past time on his own terms. So he sits in the chair next to me and asks if he can watch cartoons. We tie flies and stay current on the latest Scooby Doo series and whip up a batch of flies. I am impressed at the multi-tasking and being able to spend time with him on the vise. I happened to be tying this pattern for an upcoming trip to Alaska, and it also happened to be the first fly pattern to attract his fascination. Later that evening he coined the fly the "Shaggy Dude" most likely due to the influence of several episodes of Scooby Doo. The name stuck for the fly, and also for the material we now call "Shaggy Dub."

Adding a new material such as shaggy dub to your pattern will give you a couple of new advantages. Firstly, shaggy dubbing is one of those materials that take little to no movement from the angler to make the fly breathe with lifelike action. Even the slightest current or change in water direction creates a pulsating appearance. Secondly, shaggy dub has a sticky property and likes to tangle and weave its way around fish teeth. This increases your odds of holding a fish and making a good hook set even if you're late to detect the strike.

Target Species   Migratory and resident trout, Alaskan char and lake trout, Great Lakes steelhead/Atlantic salmon, and Pacific salmon

Favorite Color Combos   Blue/White, Pink/White, Orange/Black, Chartreuse/Blue, Chartreuse/White

THE SHAGGY DUDE MATERIALS

Shank   Flymen Fishing Company Black 40mm Senyo Steelhead/Salmon Shank (40SA-11)

Thread   White UTC 140 or Veevus 6/0 (6V-377)

Wire   Hareline Dubbin Inc. Senyo Intruder Wire or Berkley Original Fused Fireline (THW-165)

Tail   Hareline Dubbin Inc. White Marabou Blood Quill (MSBQ-377)

Body   Hareline Dubbin Inc. Pearly White Ice Dub Chenille (IDC-377)

Hackle   Enrico Puglisi Silver EP Sparkle Brush (EPE-1) and Senyo 1.5 Chromatic Live fish Brush (SCB-9)

Flash   Flashabou Rainbow (FLA-6924) or Opal Mirage Flashabou (FLA-3005)

Collar   Hareline Dubbin Inc. Natural Lady Amherst Center Tail feather (LAC-242)

Head   Hareline Dubbin Inc. Fl. Fuchsia Krystal Flash Chenille or Hot Pink Estaz (KC-131)

Eyes   Hareline Dubbing Inc. Large Pseudo dumbbell eyes (PL-Y11)

Veil   Hareline Dubbin Inc. White Senyo's Shaggy Dub (SSD-377)

THE SHAGGY DUDE TYING INSTRUCTIONS

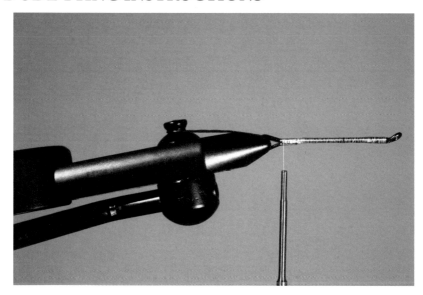

Step 1   Place a Black 40mm Senyo Steelhead Shank from Flymen Fishing Company in your vise. Attach your UTC 140 or Veevus 6/0 thread and evenly coat the entire shank and close both front and rear loops with a thin base of thread. Cut off a 4-inch piece of Senyo's Intruder Wire or 30-pound Berkley Fireline and secure it to both sides of the shank with several thread wraps. Take the tag ends through the bottom of the front loop and fold over the top of the shank. Pull tight over the top of the shank and tie down securely with several even thread wraps. Adding glue for strength is optional. Your wire loop length should not exceed 2 inches in total length.

Step 2   Wind your thread back to the rear of the shank and tie in a white marabou blood quill feather. I double check each feather and pull out the top portion of the stem to allow the feather to breathe easier and obtain more movement from the water current. Tie in six to eight strands of rainbow Flashabou over the top of the marabou tail.

Step 3   Tie in a 3-inch piece of Senyo's Baitfish 1.5 Chromatic Brush and a 3-inch piece of Enrico Puglisi's Silver Sparkle Brush. You will need to trim off one side of the sparkle brush for this step. After both brushes are tied in, leave them to hang over the marabou and toward the rear of the hook. Tie in a 3-inch piece of Pearly White Ice Dub Chenille and wind a body toward the front of the shank and secure the chenille with several thread wraps.

Step 4   Pull up and tight on both the sparkle and the chromatic brushes. Wet and stoke all the fibers from both brushes toward the rear with a little bit of moisture on your fingers, and start wrapping forward the two materials in unison and evenly spaced toward the front. You should only need four or five wraps. Secure both brushes with several thread wraps and trim away any excess. Take a wire brush or a needle and lightly comb out and pick out any stuck materials.

Step 5   Take and cut off roughly an inch worth of natural lady Amherst feather. Then place the feathers on top and secure with a loose loop of tying thread and spin the feathers evenly around the shank to form a collar. The Amherst collar should finish out at roughly 1½–2 inches in length. Add six to eight strands of rainbow Flashabou over top of the collar and make several wraps of thread to secure everything tightly in place.

Step 6   Attach a large Hareline Dubbin Inc. Tungsten Predator Eye to the bottom of the shank and secure with several figure-8 wraps and a drop of glue. Tie in a 4-inch piece of Hot Pink Krystal Flash Chenille behind the predator eyes. Make several wraps around the eyes with your chenille to form the head and secure. Trim excess material.

Step 7   Take a generous clump of Senyo's white Shaggy Dub out of the package and trim both ends of the clump to make the material even on both sides. You may need to use your scissors and cut open any extra loops of material as well. Spread the material evenly on the side you plan on tying the shaggy dub. By doing this, it should expose the center of the material and allow you to push the shaggy dubbing onto the shank. Secure the shaggy dubbing in the center with several thread wraps. After this step, simply fold over the other half of the shaggy dubbing and bring your thread to the front. Firmly hold and stroke back the material and add a drop of super glue to the base of the shaggy dubbing. Both Loon Flow and Clear Cure Goo Hydro products will work in the same manner as super glue. To finish, just build a small thread head and tie off.

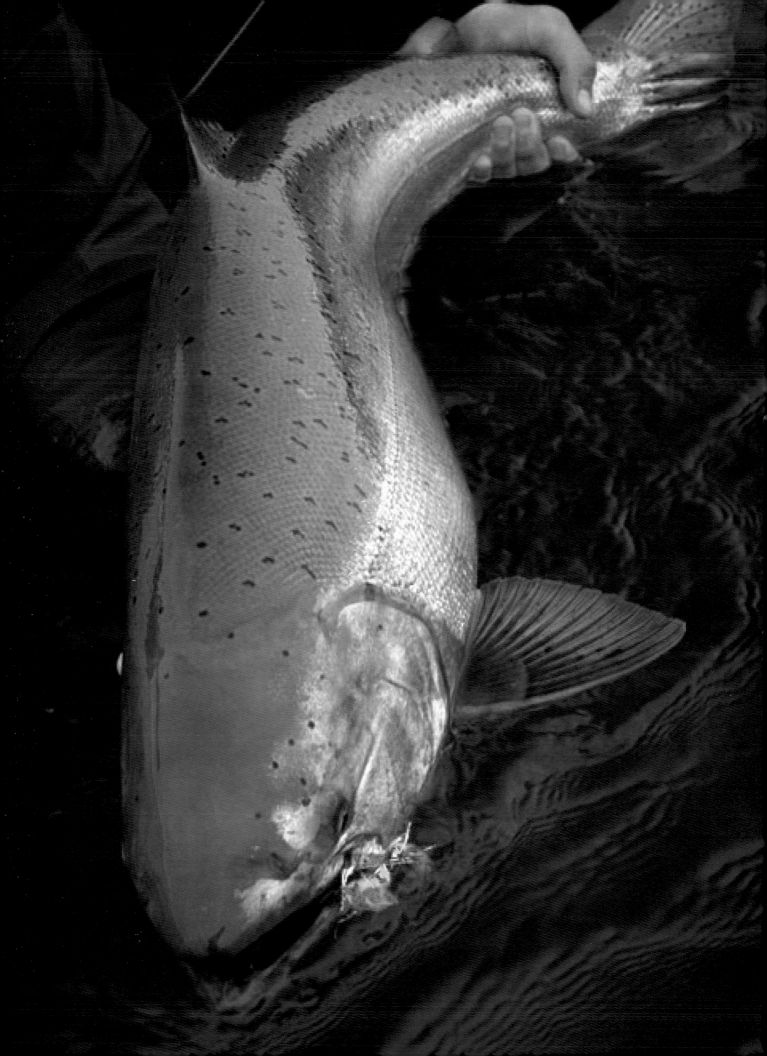

WACKO HACKLE SALMON INTRUDER

I f you have ever been lucky enough to see inside the mouth of a king salmon and the rows of teeth they possess, you will understand how quickly they can rip through your fly patterns. Durability is the name of the game for me here. I first saw the idea for tying a hinged shank intruder while fun tying with Justin Pribanic at a local Great Lakes fly shop. Now with the addition of several lengths, gauges, and color ranges of shanks offered by Flymen Fishing Company, tiers can easily adapt, articulate, or enhance their favorite patterns or create variants of their own.

By eliminating materials such as marabou, ostrich, and rhea, and replacing them with materials such as wacko hackle you can still get the fishy movement you need, instantly incorporate a moderate amount of flash, and build an extremely durable fly. This type of synthetic material also allows you to build big fly profiles without bulk. With the addition of two shanks it doubles the pattern's vertical movements and adds just the right amount of extra weight. Typically these flies will take a beating, and can serve as a multi-fisheries fly that travels well and can be adapted to catch multiple salmon species under various river conditions.

Target Species   Migratory trout, Alaskan King salmon, and Great Lakes steelhead/salmon

Favorite Color Combos   Blue/Chartreuse, Pearl/Chartreuse, Purple/Hot Orange, White/Rainbow, and Olive/Copper.

WACKO HACKLE SALMON INTRUDER MATERIALS

Rear Shank   25mm Black Flymen Fishing Company Senyo Articulated Steelhead/Salmon Shank (25SA-11)

Thread   UTC 70 or Veevus 8/0 Chartreuse (U70-54)

Wire   Senyo Black Intruder Trailer Hook Wire or Berkley Original Fused Fireline (THW-23)

Hot Butt   Hareline Dubbin Inc. Chartreuse Krystal Flash Chenille (KC-54)

Underwing   Enrico Puglisi King Fisher Blue 1.5 Short EP Foxy Brush (FXS-199)

Wing 1   Senyo's Blue Wacko Hackle (WH-23)

Wing 2   Hareline Dubbin Inc. Chartreuse Lady Amherst Center Tail Feather (LAC-54)

Rear Collar   Hareline Dubbin Inc. King Fisher Blue Guinea Feather (SGF-199)

Head   Hareline Dubbin Inc. Chartreuse Flat Diamond Braid (FD-54)

Shank 2   40mm Black Flymen Fishing Company Senyo Articulated Steelhead/Salmon Shank (40SA-11)

Body   Lagartun Chartreuse French Braid or Hareline Dubbin Inc. Chartreuse Flat Diamond Braid (FD-54)

Thorax   Hareline Dubbin Inc. Chartreuse Krystal Flash Chenille (KC-54)

Weight   Hareline Dubbin Inc. Large Senyodelic Blue Bead Chain (SBCM-23)

Underwing   Enrico Puglisi King Fisher Blue 3.0 wide EP Foxy Brush (EFX-199)

Wing 1   Senyo's Blue Wacko Hackle (WH-23)

Wing 2   Hareline Dubbin Inc. Chartreuse Lady Amherst Center Tail Feather (LAC-54)

Collar   Hareline Dubbin Inc. King Fisher Blue Guinea Feather (SGF-199)

Eye   Jungle Cock or Hareline Dubbin Inc. Real Fake Jungle Cock (FJ-5)

Hook   Partridge, Daiichi, Owner, Gamakatsu 2–4 Intruder Style (D2557)

WACKO HACKLE SALMON INTRUDER TYING INSTRUCTIONS

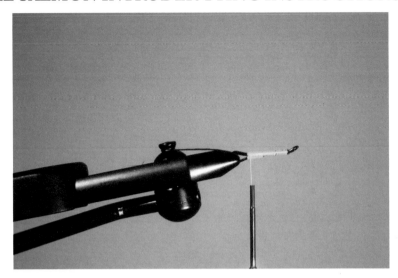

Step 1   Place a Black 25mm Senyo Steelhead Shank from Flymen Fishing Company in your vise. Attach your UTC 70 or Veevus 8/0 thread and evenly coat the entire shank and close both front and rear loops with a thin base of thread. Cut off a 4-inch piece of Senyo's Intruder Wire or 30-pound Berkley Fireline and secure it to both sides of the shank with several thread wraps. Take the tag ends through the bottom of the front loop and fold over the top of the shank. Pull tight over the top of the shank and tie down securely with several even thread wraps. Adding glue for strength is optional. Your wire loop length should not exceed 2 inches in total length.

Step 2   Wind your thread back to the rear of the shank and tie in a 2-inch piece of Hareline's Chartreuse Krystal flash Chenille. Wind the chenille until it covers the rear section of the shank where the two wires meet and come together. Secure the chenille with several thread wraps and cut off the excess. Take and cut off a 3-inch section of Enrico Puglisi 1.5 Short King Fisher Blue Foxy brush and attach to the shank in front of the chenille. Wet your fingers with some water and primp the fibers back. Palmer the brush forward with three to four wraps and secure. Cut off the remaining material and make sure the wire is pushed down flat.

Step 3   Take twenty strands of Chartreuse Lady Amherst Tail Feather roughly 2 inches long and tie them in evenly around the foxy brush. Make sure to tie this group of feathers so that all open areas are evenly covering 365 degrees around the shank.

Step 4   Take twenty strands of Blue Senyo Wacko Hackle roughly 3 inches long and tie them in evenly around the foxy brush. Make sure to tie this group of hackle to also evenly cover 365 degrees around the shank.

Step 5   Palmer a nice rear collar with a Baby Blue guinea feather, by tying the feather in by the tip so that the curve of the feather is facing down over top of the fly. This should look like an upside-down boat. Slowly wind the guinea toward the eye while pulling back on the feather fibers so they don't become tangled in each wrap. I typically wrap around the shank four times and tie off, but you can go thicker by adding a couple extra wraps. If you would like a thinner profile you can also strip one side of the guinea and the tie it in following the same steps. Attach a 1-inch piece of Chartreuse Flat Diamond Braid in front of the guinea collar and secure. Evenly wrap the flat diamond braid toward the eye of the shank, secure with several thread wraps and tie off.

Step 6   Attach the completed rear shank to a Black 40mm Senyo Steelhead Shank from Flymen Fishing Company by the rear loop and secure the 40mm shank in your vise. Attach your UTC 70 or Veevus 8/0 thread and evenly coat the entire shank and close both front and rear loops with a thin base of thread.

Step 7 Attach a 4-inch piece of Chartreuse Flat Diamond Braid and evenly wrap the flat diamond braid toward the point on the shank where the two wires form to make the eye and secure with several thread wraps.

Step 8 Attach a set of four Large Blue Senyodelic bead chain eyes to the bottom off the shank where the front two wires meet to form the shank eye and secure with several figure eight thread wraps. You can add a drop of super glue to the middle of the eyes for added strength. Cut off another 3-inch piece of the Chartreuse Krystal flash chenille and make a figure-eight wrap around the bead chain eyes.

Step 9   Take a 3-inch piece of Enrico Puglisi's Purple 3.0 wide King Fisher Blue Foxy brush and tie in front the Senyodelic bead chain. Palmer several wraps in front of the eyes to form a solid underwing. You can take a brush and comb out the fox fibers and evenly disperse the brush around the shank.

Step 10   Take twenty strands of Chartreuse Lady Amherst Tail Feather roughly 3 inches long and tie them in evenly around the foxy brush. Make sure to tie this group of feathers so that all open areas are evenly covering 365 degrees around the shank. Take twenty strands of Blue Senyo Wacko Hackle roughly 4 inches long and tie them in evenly around the foxy brush. Make sure to tie this group of hackle to also evenly cover 365 degrees around the shank.

Step 11   Add a set of Hareline's Real Fake Jungle Cock and Palmer a nice collar with a Baby Blue Guinea feather, by tying the feather in by the tip so that the curve of the feather is facing down over top of the fly. This should look like an upside-down boat. Slowly wind the guinea toward the eye while pulling back on the feather fibers so they don't become tangled in each wrap. I typically wrap around the shank four times and tie off, but you can go thicker by adding a couple extra wraps. If you would like a thinner profile you can also strip one side of the guinea and the tie it in following the same steps.

15

CITY CHICKEN

The City Chicken is another pattern based off the simple and beautiful Temple Dog and Scandinavian-style salmon flies. The difference between this version and others you see in the book is the ostrich wing. These feather plumes are readily available and typically quite long. Instead of looking for plumes that narrow and become very skinny, I look for individual plumes that are full and wide. I like the wide plumes for this pattern because the feather fibers catch more water, which translates into more erratic movements.

The cool thing is that very few feathers are needed to form the entire overwing, and a single full ostrich plume can get you a solid amount of finished flies. A lot of the time I will tie this pattern with just a white wing. This way I can adapt to several baitfish color variations by coloring the wing or creating markings with copic markers streamside. Using simple chenille, Fusion dubbing, and Predator wrap creates a stiff, yet highly translucent underbody that has the scaling and micro-spotting many baitfish have, and that was very difficult to imitate until now. Try to always keep in mind to use ostrich plumes in the wing that are light in color or that are capable of taking marker colors that are visible. If you tie this with a dark-colored ostrich wing, you will lose the ability to add color and make streamside alterations.

Target Species   Migratory and resident trout, Alaskan rainbow and char, Pacific salmon, and Great Lakes steelhead

Favorite Colors   Black/White, Black/Blue, Purple/Pink, Olive/Chartreuse, and Tan/Yellow

CITY CHICKEN MATERIALS

Rear Shank   25mm Black Flymen Fishing Company Senyo Articulated Steelhead/Salmon Shank (25SA-11)

Thread   Black UTC 70 or Veevus 8/0 (8V-11)

Shank   40mm Black Flymen Fishing Company Senyo Steelhead/Salmon Shank (40SA-11)

Loop   Senyo's Intruder Wire or Berkley Original Fused Fireline (THW-11)

Hot Spot Tag   Hareline Dubbin Inc. FL. Shrimp Pink Fine Carded Chenille (CHF-140)

Body   Senyo's Midnight Fusion Dub (FUS8)

Hackle   Senyo's UV Barred Predator Wrap (BPW2)

Under Body   Senyo's Midnight Fusion Dub (FUS8)

Wing   Hareline Dubbin In. White Ostrich Herl Plumes (OH-377)

Markings   Black Copic Sketch Marker (CSK-11)

Flash   Pearl Lateral Scale or Standard Pearl Flashabou (LSC-1703)

Collar 1   Hareline Dubbin Inc. Black Arctic Fox Tail (AFT-11)

Collar 2   Hareline Dubbin Inc. Natural Silver Pheasant Body feather (SPF-242)

Eyes   Jungle cock or Hareline Dubbin Inc. Real Fake Jungle Cock Eyes (FJ-5)

Hook   Partridge, Daiichi, Owner, Gamakatsu size 2–4 Intruder Style (D2557)

CITY CHICKEN TYING INSTRUCTIONS

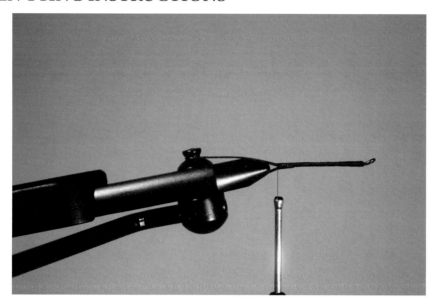

Step 1   Place a Black 40mm Senyo Steelhead Shank from Flymen Fishing Company in your vise. Attach your UTC 70 or Veevus 8/0 thread and evenly coat the entire shank and close both front and rear loops with a thin base of thread. Cut off a 4-inch piece of Senyo's Intruder Wire or 30-pound Berkley Fireline and secure it to both sides of the shank with several thread wraps. Take the tag ends through the bottom of the front loop and fold over the top of the shank. Pull tight over the top of the shank and tie down securely with several even thread wraps. Adding glue for strength is optional. Your wire loop length should not exceed 2 inches in total length.

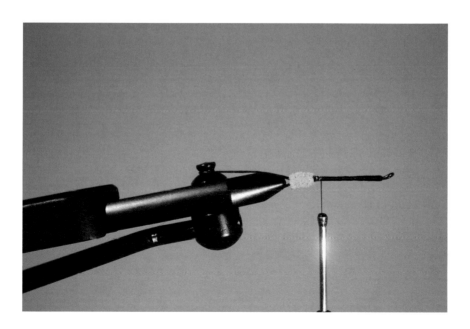

Step 2   Wind your thread back to the rear of the shank and tie in a 1-inch section of the shrimp pink fine chenille. Wrap the chenille forward until it covers the section of the shank where the two wires meet and secure with several thread wraps.

Step 3 Tie in a 4-inch piece of Senyo's UV Barred Predator wrap and let it lay out the rear. Before you tie the wrap in, prep it on a flat surface. Make sure all the predator wrap strands are not tangled and flowing in the same direction. Take your scissors and starting at the bottom cut a taper from 1–3 inches. This will basically look like an upside down half of a triangle. After you have prepped and tied in the predator wrap off the back, take a sparse amount of midnight fusion dub and make the body.

Step 4 Take a Copic or Sharpie marker and color the white cord of the Predator wrap black to match the brush color. Palmer in the Predator wrap the same way with the fibers flowing toward the rear and by the short end of the taper. After five or six evenly-spaced wraps you should secure with several thread wraps and trim away any excess materials. Take a wire brush and lightly comb out any stuck materials.

Step 5   Take a clump of midnight fusion dub and center tie it in around the shank just in front of the predator wrap. Take a wire brush and firmly comb out fibers to give it a brush appearance.

Step 6   Tie in twelve to fifteen white ostrich herl plumes over the top of the dubbing. The plumes should be 4–5 inches in length. Take your black Copic marker and evenly bar the plumes and allow a few seconds to dry. Take three individual strands of Pearl Lateral Scale Flashabou and center tie them in on the top of the wing. Fold over the Flashabou and secure with several thread wraps.

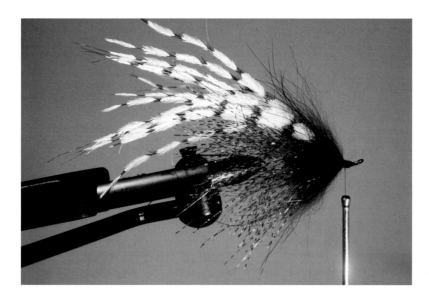

Step 7   Tie in a sparse collar of black arctic fox tail that is roughly 1½ inches long. Do not remove the guard hairs or under fur during this step. Palmer a nice collar with Hareline Dubbin Inc. Natural Silver Pheasant feather, by tying the feather in by the tip so that the curve of the feather is facing down over top of the fly. This should look like an upside-down boat. Slowly wind the Pheasant toward the eye while pulling back on the feather fibers so they don't become tangled in each wrap. Add a set of Jungle Cock Eyes, or a set of Hareline's Real Fake Jungle Cock. This is optional and is not required to finish off the pattern, but is preferred... I have found that fishing patterns with a very visible eye can be a trigger on predatory fish such as steelhead, salmon, and trout.

Step 8   Palmer a nice collar with Hareline Dubbin Inc. Natural Silver Pheasant feather, by tying the feather in by the tip so that the curve of the feather is facing down over top of the fly. This should look like an upside-down boat. Slowly wind the Pheasant toward the eye while pulling back on the feather fibers so they don't become tangled in each wrap. Add a set of Jungle Cock Eyes, or a set of Hareline's Real Fake Jungle Cock. This is optional and is not required to finish off the pattern, but is preferred. I have found that fishing patterns with a very visible eye can be a trigger on predatory fish such as steelhead, salmon, and trout.

16

BEAVER TAIL MAKUTA

The matuka is another longtime fly pattern that was a staple in my youth. I can't tell you how many brook and brown trout from the Alleghany Mountain region of Pennsylvania that fell for this simple but extremely effective fly. Over the years I tied variations of the matuka with everything from feathers, to rabbit zonker, to pine squirrel strips.

It wasn't until craft fur was released that I was able to finally find a material with fibers long enough for cutting strips to create larger versions with incredible swimming action. To use craft fur in this fly still takes a little preparation and treatment of the artificial hide. Since the craft fur is woven together, when you cut it into thin strips it has the tendency to unravel and fall apart. I take products such as Clear Cure Goo Hydro or Loon Outdoors flow and treat the entire hide with a light brushing and allow the epoxy to slightly soak into the weave. After a quick hit with a UV light, you can take a straight razor and cut the fur into long strips for tying. This is an easy way to provide the durability needed without sacrificing the properties of the long fur.

Today I use this variant of the matuka for everything including Great Lakes steelhead, trout, and smallmouth bass. The Beaver Tail Matuka is another example of adding an historic fly pattern to your fly box by simply adjusting the materials to create a variant suitable for your fishery.

Target Species   Migratory and resident trout, Alaskan rainbow, char, and Pacific salmon, and Great Lakes steelhead, salmon, and smallmouth bass

Favorite Colors   Orange/Gold, Lavender/Blue, Black/Purple, Red/Black, and Olive/Chartreuse

BEAVER TAIL MAKUTA MATERIALS

Thread   Black UTC 70 or Veevus 8/0 (U70-380)

Shank   40mm Black Flymen Fishing Company Senyo Steelhead/Salmon Shank (40SA-11)

Loop   Senyo's Intruder Wire or Berkley Original Fused Fireline (THW-11)

Tag   Hareline Gold Flat Diamond Braid (FD-344)

Body   Hareline Red Flat Diamond Braid (FD-310)

Rib   Veevus Gold Medium French Tinsel (VTM-153)

Under Wing   Senyo's Chocolate Covered Cherry Aqua Veil (SA2)

Wing   Hareline Dubbin Inc. Black Extra Select Craft Fur (XCF-11)

Collar   Hareline Dubbin Inc. Red Strung Silver Pheasant Body feather (SPF-310)

Eyes   Jungle cock or Hareline Dubbin Inc. Real Fake Jungle Cock Eyes (FJ-5)

Hook   Partridge, Daiichi, Owner, Gamakatsu size 2–4 Intruder Style (D2557)

BEAVER TAIL MAKUTA TYING INSTRUCTIONS

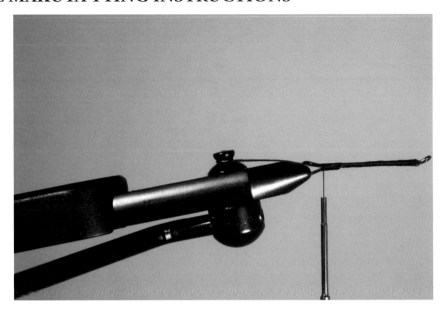

Step 1   Place a Black 40mm Senyo Steelhead Shank from Flymen Fishing Company in your vise. Attach your UTC 70 or Veevus 8/0 thread and evenly coat the entire shank and close both front and rear loops with a thin base of thread. Cut off a 4-inch piece of Senyo's Intruder Wire or 30-pound Berkley Fireline and secure it to both sides of the shank with several thread wraps. Take the tag ends through the bottom of the front loop and fold over the top of the shank. Pull tight over the top of the shank and tie down securely with several even thread wraps. Adding glue for strength is optional. Your wire loop length should not exceed 2 inches in total length.

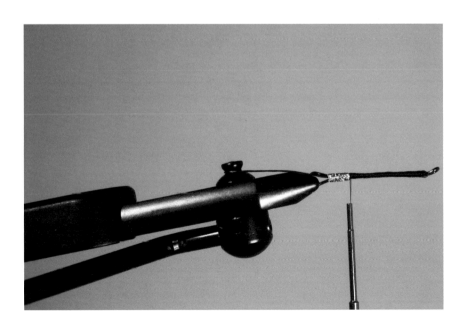

Step 2   Wind your thread back to the rear of the shank and tie in a 1-inch section of Gold flat Diamond braid. Wrap the flat braid forward until it covers the section of the shank where the two wires meet and secure with several thread wraps.

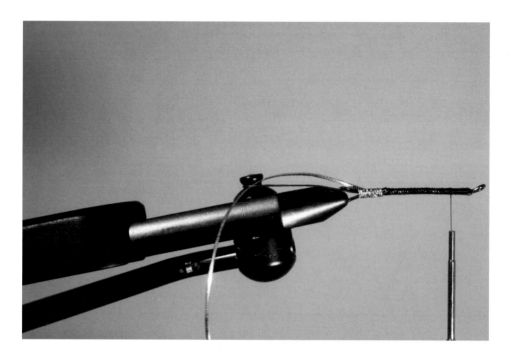

Step 3 Tie in a 3-inch piece of red flat diamond braid and a 3-inch piece of Veevus medium gold French tinsel. Evenly wrap the mini flat braid toward the eye of the shank stopping where the two wires are bent and meet to form the eye. Take the Veevus French tinsel and just allow it to hang off the back for tying steps still to come.

Step 4 Take a cut a ⅛-inch wide strip of Hareline's Black Extra Select Craft Fur, roughly 4 inches of the artificial hide will remain with about a 6-inch wing. Coat the bottom of the hide with Loon's Flow fly Finish and dry with a UV light. This step will keep the hide from unraveling and losing fur fibers while fishing. Tie in the Craft Fur strip so that the hide length is roughly twice the length of the shank and secure.

Step 5   Take the hanging piece of Veevus French Tinsel and evenly wrap the tinsel through the craft fur strip and secure by pulling up tightly on the tinsel before locking it down with tying thread. Trim away any excess Craft Fur.

Step 6   Tie in a 4-inch piece of Senyo's Chocolate Covered Cherry Aqua Veil, and palmer the aqua veil forward with the fibers all flowing toward the rear of the shank. Wetting the fibers of the aqua veil before winding forward with a little bit of water on your fingers will make this step a breeze.

Step 7   Palmer a nice collar with Hareline Dubbin Inc. Red Strung Silver Pheasant Body feather, by tying the feather in by the tip so that the curve of the feather is facing down over top of the fly. This should look like an upside-down boat. Slowly wind the feather toward the eye while pulling back on the feather fibers so they don't become tangled in each wrap. I typically wrap around the shank four times and tie off, but you can go thicker by adding a couple extra wraps. If you would like a thinner profile you can also strip one side of the feather and the tie it in following the same steps.

Step 8   You can add a set of Jungle Cock Eyes, or a set of Hareline's Real Fake Jungle Cock. This is optional and is not required to finish off the pattern, but is preferred... I have found that fishing patterns with a very visible eye can be a trigger on predatory fish such as steelhead, salmon, and trout.

17

SWINGER'S HEX

I f you have never had an opportunity to experience the "big bug" hatches of the east and Midwest, you need to add it to your bucket list. The nice thing is that the nymph stage offers a meaty subsurface feast, and the hex nymph has been highly imitated by Midwestern anglers for years. Even the fabled Eastern Green Drakes fit well into this pattern's fishing range. Swinging soft hackles and wet flies has long been an American pastime, but with the recent adoption of Skagit casting and microspey options for trout over the past years, the Swinger's Hex is a very easy and practical fly that covers the big mayfly appearance, but also is very imitative of a small darter or creek chub. We all enjoy the watching trout eat off the surface, but swinging up a trout has become a very close second and a great way to stay fresh on your two-handed casting all year long.

I've always looked at the latest materials to form a very distinct and pronounced wing case. On this pattern and on most all of my hex and drake imitations, I like to use vinyl flooring and the crazy color concoctions created for modern homes. They are cheap and easy to secure, as all major hardware stores sell small color samples. I like to trim them to size and hit them with a copic or Sharpie marker to enhance the 3D ridges and marbling most vinyl already has. The use of vinyl is also extremely useful when constructing any type of fly imitation where a shellback or wing case is needed.

Target Species   Migratory and resident trout, and Great Lakes steelhead

Favorite Color Combos   Cream, Olive, Brown, Tan, Gray, White, Yellow, and Black

SWINGER'S HEX MATERIALS

Rear Shank   25mm Black Flymen Fishing Company Senyo Articulated Steelhead/Salmon Shank (25SA-11)

Shank   Flymen Fishing Company Copper 25mm Senyo Steelhead/Salmon Shank (25SA-271)

Thread   UTC 70 or Veevus 10/0 FL. Rusty Brown (10V-323)

Wire   Hareline Dubbin Inc. Senyo Intruder Wire or Berkley Original Fused Fireline (SIW-11)

Tail   Hareline Dubbin Inc. Cream Marabou Blood Quill (MSBQ-72)

Tail 2   Hareline Dubbin Inc. Tan Lady Amherst Center Tail Feather (LAC-369)

Underbody   Hareline Dubbin Inc. Cream Marabou Blood Quill (MSBQ-72)

Rib   Veevus Gold Medium French Tinsel (VTM-153)

Hackle   Hareline Dubbin Inc. Grizzly or Fiery Brown Schlappen Feather (SCHL-114)

Wing Pads   Vinyl Floor Piece Mottled Tan or Marbled Mustard color

Markings   Copic Brown Sketch Marker (CSK-40)

Eyes   Hareline Dubbin Inc. Small Black Bead Chain Eyes (BCS-11)

Hook   Partridge, Gamakatsu, or Owner size 4–6 Intruder style hook (D2557)

SWINGER'S HEX TYING INSTRUCTIONS

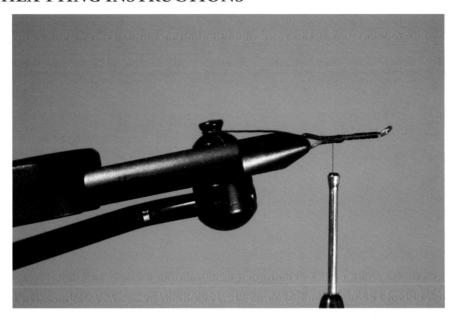

Step 1 Place a copper 25mm Senyo Steelhead Shank from Flymen Fishing Company in your vise. Attach your UTC 70 or Veevus 10/0 thread and evenly coat the entire shank and close both front and rear loops with a thin base of thread. Cut off a 4-inch piece of Senyo's Intruder Wire or 30-pound Berkley Fireline and secure it to both sides of the shank with several thread wraps. Take the tag ends through the bottom of the front loop and fold over the top of the shank. Pull tight over the top of the shank and tie down securely with several even thread wraps. Adding glue for strength is optional. Your wire loop length should not exceed 2 inches in total length.

Step 2 Tie in a Cream Marabou blood Quill plume and three strands of tan lady Amherst center tail feather over the top. Remove the top portion of the center stem in the cream marabou before tying in.

Step 3   Tie in a 1-inch piece of Veevus Medium gold French tinsel and allow it to hang off the back. Take the remains of the Cream marabou blood quill and dub a short body with the feather plumes. Take your tinsel and make two to three even wraps to rib the short body.

Step 4   Tie in a webby 5–7 inch long Schlappen feather by the tip and let it lay over the top of the marabou. Next grab a small piece of vinyl flooring. I typically store these as 3 × 3-inch sheets in my tying bin. Take and cut off a ¼ × ¼ inch square of our vinyl sheet. Cut out a "v" shape on one end and trim the edges of the opposite end to make the wing pad. Tie in the vinyl by the point.

Step 5   After the first vinyl wing pad is in place, make a couple wraps with your Schlappen and secure. Repeat the same process on building the wing pad for step number two. I typically know I will be needing three wing pads made, so I will prep out the number I need to cover how many flies I will be tying in advance.

Step 6   Once the second wing pad is in place and the Schlappen has been brought to the front, tie is a small set of black bead chain eyes to the bottom of the shank and secure with several figure eight wraps. Palmer the Schlappen through and around the eyes to make a collar and secure. Place the third and final wing pad on top over the eyes and Schlappen collar. Trim off any excess vinyl and build a nice thread head.

Step 7   Cut off the tying thread and touch up the vinyl wing pads with a brown Copic sketch marker and allow to dry.

18

FUSION FRY

No matter where you fish if you are any place fry are schooled up and present, you can be certain predators are close by. Fishing fry imitations can offer some of the most exciting streamer fishing of the season. The fry hatch and rainbow fishing in Alaska is mesmerizing, the salmon fry hatches on many Great Lakes tributaries put the feedbag on big and otherwise wary trout.

The Fusion Fry is as simple to tie as it gets, four materials and a light trim and you are off and running. By using the updated chromatic brushes from Enrico Puglisi and a sparse amount of dubbing you can build a 3-D and translucent minnow profile in a single step, with no extra flash materials needed to form the body.

The best part is this pattern is nearly impossible to screw up and a very simple way to match the hatch and fill your box in a timely manner. I tend to use a lot of copic or Sharpie permanent markers to enhance this fly, by barring and spotting the brushes to imitate the natural.

Target Species   Migratory and resident trout, Alaskan char, Great Lakes steelhead, Pacific and Great Lakes salmon Species, and resident river or migratory smallmouth bass.

Favorite Color Combos   Olive, Chartreuse, Black, Blue, Tan, and White.

FUSION FRY MATERIALS

Shank   Flymen Fishing Company Black 25mm Senyo Steelhead/Salmon Shank (25SA-11)

Thread   UTC 70 or Veevus 10/0 White (10V-377)

Wire   Hareline Dubbin Inc. Senyo Intruder Wire or Berkley Original Fused Fireline (SIW-165)

Wing   EP Senyo Erie Emerald 3.0 Wide Chromatic Brush (WSC-6)

Markings   Black Copic Sketch Marker (CSK-11

Thorax   Senyo Shrimp Pink Laser Dub (SL-340)

Head   Senyo Emerald Fusion Dubbing (FUS-4)

Gills   Red Copic Sketch Marker (CSK-310)

Eyes   Hareline Dubbin Inc. 3D Adhesive Holographic Eyes (33D-344)

Hook   Partridge, Gamakatsu, or Owner size 2–4 Intruder style hook (D2557)

FUSION FRY TYING INSTRUCTIONS

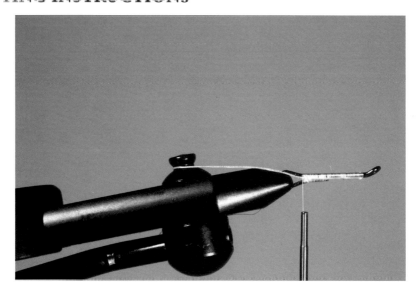

Step 1 Place a Black 25mm Senyo Steelhead Shank from Flymen Fishing Company in your vise. Attach your UTC 70 or Veevus 10/0 thread and evenly coat the entire shank and close both front and rear loops with a thin base of thread. Cut off a 4-inch piece of Senyo's Intruder Wire or 30-pound Berkley Fireline and secure it to both sides of the shank with several thread wraps. Take the tag ends through the bottom of the front loop and fold over the top of the shank. Pull tight over the top of the shank and tie down securely with several even thread wraps. Adding glue for strength is optional. Your wire loop length should not exceed 2 inches in total length.

Step 2 Tie in a 3-inch piece of Erie Emerald 3.0 Chromatic brush and make six to eight wraps forward to form a compact and tight ball of material around the shank. You should wrap the brush to the point on the shank were the two wires meet to form the eye of the shank. An easy way to get the foxy brush to fold back and fibers to flow the same direction is to get them wet and pull back tight on the fibers while you are winding forward. Take a needle or a wire brush and pick or comb out the material so it flows nicely to the rear of the shank.

Step 3   To tie in the thorax grab a pinch of Laser dubbing and pull them apart until you get all the dubbing fibers flowing in the same direction. From here rotate your vise and tie in the laser dubbing in at the center of the clump with several thread wraps. The remaining laser dubbing is then folded over onto itself and your thread brought to the front. After this step, rotate your vise 180 degrees back to its upright position.

Step 4   To tie in the head grab a pinch of Erie Emerald Fusion dubbing and pull them apart until you get all the dubbing fibers flowing in the same direction. Once again center tie the fusion dub and fold the fibers toward the rear and lock in with several thread wraps.

Step 5   To finish off the fry, make a rough scissor trim along the bottom and sides of the pattern to create a bullet-shaped profile. Attach a set of Hareline 3DHolographic eyes by applying a drop of Super Glue or Loctite gel to the head and pressing down firmly to lock the eyes to the materials. Take a black copic marker and make four or five light bars on the chromatic brush wing, and then a small gill plate with a red copic sketch marker. *Note:* Crazy Glue is now available with a brush allowing clean and easy application. I rarely whip finish and mainly use just a quick half hitch anymore. The glue as a finish application to the thread is stronger than any knot you can tie.

ELECTRICAL TAPE STONE

This has quickly become a low-water favorite for me—nearly every tributary I cross has some type of stonefly population. I tend to over-exaggerate the size and totally change the traditional stonefly pattern to better fit my personality and preferred fishing tendencies. This pattern can be adapted to a standard hook if you prefer to dead drift, as opposed to swimming the fly.

The key for me is just to impersonate food: The extra-long rubber legs provide just the right amount of movement for low or clear water presentations. The wing case has a similar construction to the wing pads for the Swinger's Hex. The major difference is that I use electrical tape to create the distinct stonefly exoskeleton. The tape is soft and another extremely durable tying substitute. A single roll of electrical tape will last you a lifetime of Electrical Tape Stone flies.

Target Species   Migratory brown trout, Alaskan char, Great Lakes and PNW steelhead, Pacific and Great Lakes salmon species, and smallmouth bass.

Favorite Color Combos   Cream, Olive, Brown, Tan, Gray, White, Yellow, and Black

ELECTRICAL TAPE STONE MATERIALS

Shank   Flymen Fishing Company Blue 25mm Senyo Steelhead/Salmon Shank (25SA-23)

Thread   UTC 70 or Veevus 10/0 Black (10V-11)

Wire   Hareline Dubbin Inc. Senyo Intruder Wire or Berkley Original Fused Fireline (THW-11)

Tail   Hareline Dubbin Inc. Blue/Black Fly Enhancer Legs (FE-23)

Body   Hareline Dubbin Inc. Black Flat Diamond Braid (FD-11)

Legs   Hareline Dubbin Inc. Blue/Black Fly Enhancer Legs (FE-23)

Thorax   Senyo Midnight Fusion Dub (FUS-8)

Wing Pads   Black Electrical tape

Eyes   Hareline Dubbin Inc. Senyodelic Medium Bead Chain (SBCM-23)

Hook   Partridge, Gamakatsu, or Owner size 2–4 Intruder style hook (D2557)

ELECTRICAL TAPE STONE TYING INSTRUCTIONS

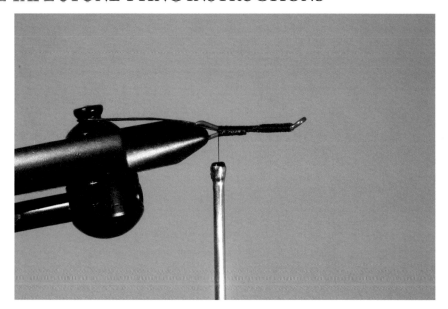

Step 1   Place a Blue 25mm Senyo Steelhead Shank from Flymen Fishing Company in your vise. Attach your UTC 70 or Veevus 10/0 thread and evenly coat the entire shank and close both front and rear loops with a thin base of thread. Cut off a 4-inch piece of Senyo's Intruder Wire or 30-pound Berkley Fireline and secure it to both sides of the shank with several thread wraps. Take the tag ends through the bottom of the front loop and fold over the top of the shank. Pull tight over the top of the shank and tie down securely with several even thread wraps. Adding glue for strength is optional. Your wire loop length should not exceed 2 inches in total length.

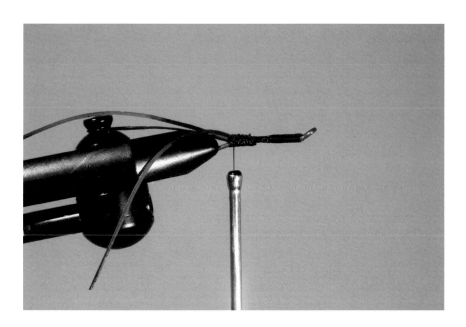

Step 2   Tie in a set of Black and blue fly enhancer rubber legs out the back of the shank. There should be one on each side of the rear loop. The length of the rubber leg tail should be just a tad longer than the 25mm shank.

Step 3   Tie in a 1-inch piece of black diamond flat braid and evenly wind forward to create an even but thin body and secure with several thread wraps. Take a single 4-inch long Black/Blue rubber leg and center tie onto both sides of the shank, so that an even amount (2 inches each) of rubber leg protrude. Take a sparse amount of midnight fusion dub and figure-8 wrap the dubbing around the rubber legs. At this point I just bring my thread to the front and use a needle to pick out some of the dub.

Step 4   Take a roll of black electrical tape and cut off a 2-inch section of tape. Fold the sticky side together to form a 1-inch square. Take and cut off a ¼ x ¼–inch square off of the Electrical tape. Cut out a "v" shape on one end and trim the edges of the opposite end to make the wing pad. Tie in the Electrical tape in by the point.

Step 5   After the first electrical tape wing pad is in place and secure, repeat the same process on building the legs and thorax you did for step number four. I typically know I will be needing three wing pads made, so I will prep out the number I need to cover how many flies I will be tying in advance.

Step 6   Once the second wing pad is in place, tie is a set of medium Senyodelic bead chain eyes to the bottom of the shank and secure with several figure eight wraps. Dub a sparse amount of midnight fusion dun around the bead chain eyes, and place the third and final wing pad on top over the eyes. Trim off any excess electrical tape and build a nice thread head.

20

CHAIN GANG INTRUDER

The construction of this Intruder/Game Changer allows its body to collapse and present a very slim and sleek appearance, almost like a lamprey, leech, or wormlike profile underwater. Most of the time we strictly try to build profile or imitate the appearance of a baitfish or other intended quarry. Sometimes we just need a fly that lives, breathes, and just constantly moves. By tying it with three separate shanks it pretty much allows it to swim like it's moving along with the action of a wave.

This is the type of pattern I love to run when nothing is going on; something that can trigger a strike response. The saying "it looks like food, acts like food, it must be food" applies to the reaction that curious fish have toward this fly. The action on this pattern is both vertical and horizontal by function, but angler manipulation such as stripping line at various speeds and jigging the rod will add secondary action and movement to the fly.

This is a pattern that takes a bit of time to construct due to the amount of components. Typically I have four or five of these in my box in various color combinations. The time is warranted and necessary if you want the intended action and fly movement the shanked body provides.

Target Species   Migratory trout, Alaskan trout/salmon, Great Lakes steelhead/salmon, and PNW steelhead

Favorite Color Combos   Blue/Chartreuse, Black/Chartreuse, Purple/Shrimp Pink, White/Rainbow, and Olive/Copper.

CHAIN GANG INTRUDER MATERIALS

Rear Shank   15mm Flymen Fishing Company Articulated Fish Spine (15FS)

Thread   UTC 70 or Veevus 8/0 Hot Orange (8V-137)

Wire   Senyo Black Intruder Trailer Hook Wire or Berkley Original Fused Fireline (THW-11)

Underwing   Senyo's Raspberry Aqua Veil (SA-11)

Wing 1   Hareline Dubbin Inc. Lavender Marabou Blood Quill (MSBQ-200)

Wing 2   Hareline Dubbin Inc. Shrimp Pink Lady Amherst Center Tail Feather (LAC-343)

Flash   Mirage Flashabou Opal/Copper (FLA-3306)

Mid Shank   20mm Flymen Fishing Company Articulated Fish Spine (20FS)

Body   Hareline Dubbin Inc. Shrimp Pink Fine Carded Chenille (CHF-140)

Front Shank   15mm Flymen Fishing Company Articulated Fish Spine (15FS)

Underwing   Senyo's Raspberry Aqua Veil (SA-11)

Wing 1   Hareline Dubbin Inc. Lavender Marabou Blood Quill (MSBQ-200)

Wing 2   Hareline Dubbin Inc. Shrimp Pink Lady Amherst Center Tail Feather (LAC-343)

Flash   Mirage Flashabou Opal/Copper (FLA-3306)

Eye   Jungle Cock or Hareline Dubbin Inc. Real Fake Jungle Cock (FJ-5)

Hook   Partridge, Daiichi, Owner, Gamakatsu size 2–4 Intruder Style (D2557)

CHAIN GANG INTRUDER TYING INSTRUCTIONS

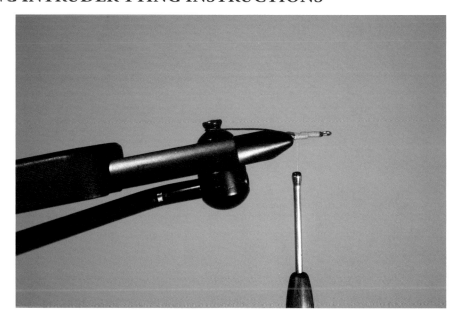

Step 1   Place a 10mm Articulated Fish Spine from Flymen Fishing Company in your vise. Attach your UTC 70 or Veevus 8/0 thread and evenly coat the entire shank and close both front and rear loops with a thin base of thread. Cut off a 4-inch piece of Senyo's Intruder Wire or 30-pound Berkley Fireline and secure it to both sides of the shank with several thread wraps. Take the tag ends through the bottom of the front loop and fold over the top of the shank. Pull tight over the top of the shank and tie down securely with several even thread wraps. Adding glue for strength is optional. Your wire loop length should not exceed 2 inches in total length.

Step 2   Wind your thread back to the rear of the shank and tie in a 2-inch piece of Raspberry Aqua Veil Chenille. Wind the chenille until it covers half of the shank.

Step 3   Take a lavender marabou feather and lightly strike the feathers down and away from the stem to expose the center. Tie in the marabou by the tip section of the center stem. I like to start roughly an inch or so into the feather as my tie point. Fold over the tip and lock it down with several thread wraps. Palmer the marabou around the shank three times to form the wing. Cut off the excess feather as tight to the shank as possible. If you wet and stroke all the feathers and stroke them toward the rear of the shank, it will simplify this step. When the plumes dry, it will fluff back out. To finish this step, add eight to ten strands of opal/copper Mirage Flashabou over the top.

Step 4   Take six to eight individual strands of Shrimp Pink Lady Amherst Tail Feather roughly 2 inches long and tie them in, spaced evenly, around the marabou. Tie off the thread and add a little glue to the head for additional strength.

Step 5 Take the completed tail out of the vise and attach it to the rear loop of a 20mm articulated fish spine. Reattach your thread and lay down a thread base and close the rear loop.

Step 6 Tie in a 2-inch piece of shrimp pink fine chenille and cover the entire shank with even wraps. Build a nice thread head, tie off, and add a drop of glue for strength.

Step 7 Take the completed sections out of the vise and attach the center shank into the rear loop of a 15mm articulated fish spine. Reattach your thread and lay down a thread base and close the rear loop.

Step 8 Wind your thread back to the rear of the shank and tie in a 2-inch piece of Raspberry Aqua Veil Chenille. Wind the chenille until it covers half of the shank.

Step 9   Take a lavender marabou feather and lightly strike the feathers down and away from the stem to expose the center. Tie in the marabou by the tip section on the center stem. I like to start roughly and inch or so into the feather as my tie point. Fold over the tip and lock it down will several thread wraps. Palmer the marabou around the shank three times to form the wing. Cut off the excess feather as tight to the shank as possible. If you wet and stroke all the feathers and stroke them toward the rear of the shank, it will simplify this step. When the plumes dry it will fluff back out. To finish this step, add eight to ten strands of opal/copper Mirage Flashabou over the top.

Step 10   Take six to eight individual strands of Shrimp Pink Lady Amherst Tail Feather roughly 2 inches long and tie them in evenly spaced around the marabou. Add a set of Hareline's Real Fake Jungle or Jungle Cock Feather. Build an even thread head and tie off.

21

TROUT TANTRUM

I grew up fishing wet flies on my local trout streams, but it wasn't until I started swinging flies for steelhead that I really put much thought on the versatility these small flies possessed. Many of my homewater steelhead streams become very low and extremely clear. Sometimes these periods would last for a very long time making tactics limited for anglers.

I started resorting back to old wet flies such as the partridge and green. The truth was it was pretty difficult to be successful at times with such small light wire hooks. I started playing with Flymen Fishing Company's

Fish Spines that added just the right size and amount of weight to improve swimming characteristics and still gain some depth. By adding the small stinger tied as a secondary wet fly I was able to represent a small brace on a sturdy and strong hook.

Due to the construction of this pattern it can be run as a single wet fly by just adding a small stinger hook to the rear, or fished as a double by adding a dressed hook. For both trout and steelhead when the conditions are tough and the water as clear as it gets, use this simple and non-intrusive pattern to cover water with wary fish.

Target Species   Resident trout and low-water Great Lakes steelhead.

Favorite Color Combos   Olive, Tan, Black, Brown, Gray, and White.

TROUT TANTRUM MATERIALS

Shank   20mm Flymen Fishing Company Articulated Fish Spine (20FS)

Thread   UTC 70 or Veevus 10/0 olive (10V-263)

Wire   Hareline Dubbin Inc. Senyo Intruder Wire or Berkley Original Fused Fireline (SIW-165)

Body   Veevus Gold French Tinsel (VTM-153)

Thorax   Shrimp Pink Laser Dub (SL-340)

Flash   Speckled Copper Flashabou (FLA-6934)

Wing   Natural Teal Flank Feathers (TFF-242)

Hook   Size 6 Intruder Style Hook (D2557)

Body   Veevus Gold French Tinsel (VTM-153)

Thorax   Hareline Dubbin Inc. UV Dark Olive Ice Dub (ICE-95)

Wing   Natural Teal Flank Feathers (TFF-242)

TROUT TANTRUM TYING INSTRUCTIONS

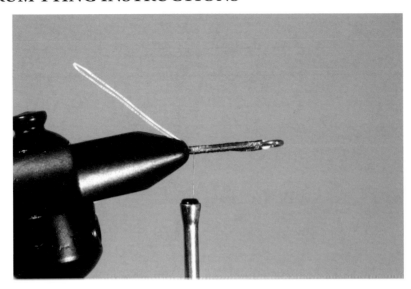

Step 1   Cut the loop off a 20mm Articulated Fish Spine from Flymen Fishing Company and place in your vise. Attach your UTC 70 or Veevus 10/0 thread and evenly coat the entire shank and close both front and rear loops with a thin base of thread. Cut off a 4-inch piece of Senyo's Intruder Wire or 30-pound Berkley Fireline and secure it to both sides of the shank with several thread wraps. Take the tag ends through the bottom of the front loop and fold over the top of the shank. Pull tight over the top of the shank and tie down securely with several even thread wraps. Adding glue for strength is optional. Your wire loop length should not exceed 2 inches in total length.

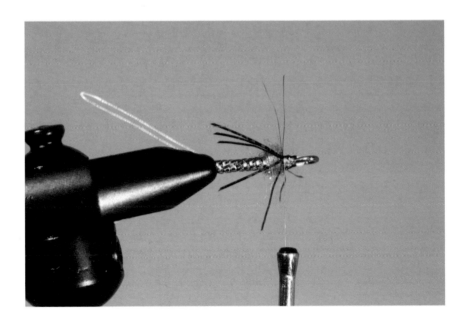

Step 2   Tie in a 3-inch piece of Veevus Gold French Tinsel and make six to eight wraps forward to form the body. To tie in the thorax, dub a sparse ball of Shrimp pink Laser dubbing. Next tie in four to five strands of speckled copper Flashabou to each side of the dubbing ball. Make sure to trim them to roughly ½ inch in length.

Step 3   Palmer a nice collar with Hareline Dubbin Inc. Natural Teal Flank Feather, by tying the feather in by the tip so that the curve of the feather is facing down over top of the fly. This should look like an upside-down boat. Slowly wind the feather toward the eye while pulling back on the feather fibers so they don't become tangled in each wrap. I typically wrap around the shank four times and tie off, but you can go thicker by adding a couple extra wraps. If you would like a thinner profile you can also strip one side of the guinea and tie it in following the same steps. Trim off any excess feather and create a uniformed thread head and tie off.

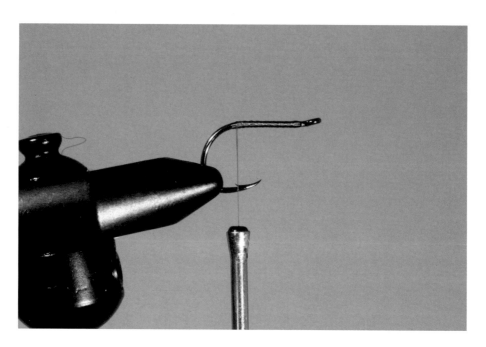

Step 4   Remove the shank from your vise and add your size 6 intruder style to the vise. Attach your thread and lay a base coat to the hook.

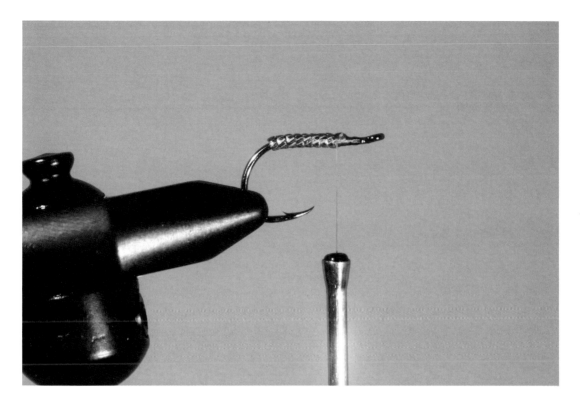

Step 5 Tie in a 3-inch piece of Veevus Gold French Tinsel and make six to eight wraps forward to form the body.

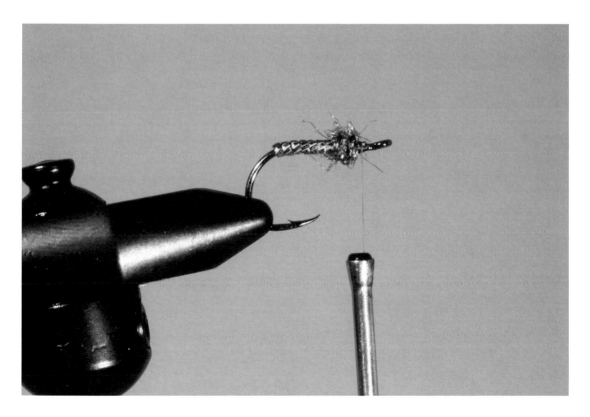

Step 6 To tie in the thorax, dub a sparse ball of UV Dark Olive Ice dubbing.

Step 7   Palmer a nice collar with Hareline Dubbin Inc. Natural Teal Flank Feather, by tying the feather in by the tip so that the curve of the feather is facing down over top of the fly. This should look like an upside-down boat. Slowly wind the feather toward the eye while pulling back on the feather fibers so they don't become tangled in each wrap. I typically wrap around the shank four times and tie off, but you can go thicker by adding a couple extra wraps. If you would like a thinner profile you can also strip one side of the guinea and tie it in following the same steps. Trim off any excess feather and create a uniformed thread head and tie off.

Step 8   To finish the pattern, take the finished hook and wet all the fibers together, take and feed the wire from the back of the shanked fly through the bottom of the hook eye. Open the loop and bring the open loop over the hook. This will loop connect the shank to the hook.

22

GROUND ZERO LEECH

Just to be up front, I don't fill my fly box with this pattern. More or less, I have two or three Ground Zero Leeches with me because water clarity and river conditions on the Great lakes change very quickly. This is the type of pattern I like to fish when our rivers become very high and flow like chocolate milk. Typically if I can't get fish to move on this fly during these conditions I hang it up or start traveling to another river system.

More times than not, I'm looking at a river on a day I can fish and it's never the best conditions. On the plus side there is nobody around to get in my way and I have the river to myself. We have to remember that fish are not leaving the river during this time, but they are moving to locations that are commonly overlooked. That overlooked place is usually straight down by your feet. The big difference about fishing this pattern is we want to start out in the faster flooded current, but want the fly to be able to swim all the way to the shore. Not close to shore, *all the way* to shore.

Instead of relying on heavy sink tips and a lot of weight to get down, I typically go very light on my tips and run a very short tippet. This way I can cast into the heavy flow and mend or move the fly accordingly to set up the fly depth and swing as it enters the shallow water. I want the fly to hover or climb along the taper of the river bottom. By adding the extra fur and mass, the Ground Zero Leech gains a weed guard and avoids getting hung up on the debris in the flow and the uneven contour of the river bottom as the fly swims into shore. Most of my fly grabs will happen in a foot of water or less, and very close to the shoreline.

Target Species   (High-water) Great Lakes steelhead, salmon, trout, and bass

Favorite Color Combos   Blue/Chartreuse, Pearl/Chartreuse, Purple/Hot Orange, White/Rainbow, and Olive/Copper.

GROUND ZERO LEECH MATERIALS

Rear Shank   25mm Black Flymen Fishing Company Senyo Articulated Steelhead/Salmon Shank (25SA-11)

Thread   UTC 70 or Veevus 8/0 Black (8V-11)

Wire   Senyo Black Intruder Trailer Hook Wire or Berkley Original Fused Fireline (THW-11)

Tail   Hareline Dubbin Inc. Chartreuse Finn Raccoon Fur (FRZ-54)

Flash   Kelly Green Flashabou (FLA-6903) and Gun Metal Flashabou (FLA-6916)

Body   Hareline Dubbin Inc. Chartreuse Diamond Flat Braid (FD-54)

Wing   Hareline Dubbin Inc. Chartreuse Finn Raccoon (FRZ-54)

Flash   Kelly Green Flashabou (FLA-6903) and Gun Metal Flashabou (FLA-6919)

Head   Chartreuse Laser dub (SL-127)

Front Shank   25mm Black Flymen Fishing Company Senyo Articulated Steelhead/Salmon (25SA-11)

Tail   Hareline Dubbin Inc. Black Finn Raccoon Fur (FRZ-11)

Body   Nuked Green Bean Aqua Veil (SA6)

Wing   Hareline Dubbin Inc. Black Finn Raccoon Fur (FRZ-11)

Rear Collar   Hareline Dubbin Inc. King Chartreuse Guinea Feather (SGF-54)

Head   Pink Lady Fusion Dub (FUS-10)

Eyes   Hareline Dubbin Inc. Large Senyodelic Blue Bead Chain (SBCM-23)

Veil   Blended Chartreuse Laser Dub (SL-127) and Emerald Green Ice Dub (ICE-110)

GROUND ZERO LEECH TYING INSTRUCTIONS

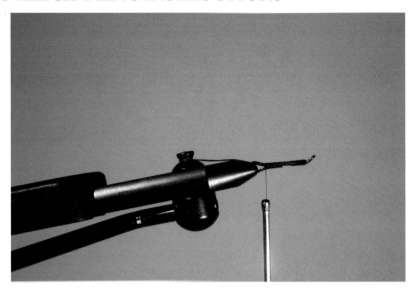

Step 1   Place a Black 25mm Senyo Steelhead Shank from Flymen Fishing Company in your vise. Attach your UTC 70 or Veevus 8/0 thread and evenly coat the entire shank and close both front and rear loops with a thin base of thread. Cut off a 4-inch piece of Senyo's Intruder Wire or 30-pound Berkley Fireline and secure it to both sides of the shank with several thread wraps. Take the tag ends through the bottom of the front loop and fold over the top of the shank. Pull tight over the top of the shank and tie down securely with several even thread wraps. Adding glue for strength is optional. Your wire loop length should not exceed 2 inches in total length.

Step 2   Wind your thread back to the rear of the shank and tie in a clump of Hareline's Chartreuse Finn Raccoon Fur. This clump of fur should equal about a marabou plume worth of material that is roughly 3 inches long. If you take your free hand you can evenly disperse the fur around the shank by simply twisting the fur with your fingers. Tie in ten to fifteen strands of both Kelly Green and Gun Metal Flashabou over top of the Finn Raccoon Tail and secure with several thread wraps.

Step 3   Attach a 3-inch piece of Chartreuse Flat Diamond Braid and evenly wrap the flat diamond braid toward the point on the shank where the two wires form to make the eye and secure with several thread wraps.

Step 4   Repeat **Step 2** and tie in a clump of Hareline's Chartreuse Finn Raccoon Fur. This clump of fur should equal about a marabou plume worth of material that is roughly 3 inches long. If you take your free hand you can evenly disperse the fur around the shank by simply twisting the fur with your fingers. Tie in ten to fifteen strands of both Kelly Green and Gun Metal Flashabou over the top of the Finn Raccoon Tail and secure with several thread wraps.

Step 5   Center tie in a clump of Chartreuse laser dubbing in front of the Finn Raccoon. Pull all the dubbing toward the rear and bring your thread to the front. Lock it down with several wraps, tie off and remove from your vise.

Step 6   Attach the Completed rear shank to a Black 25mm Senyo Steelhead Shank from Flymen Fishing Company by the rear loop and secure the 40mm shank in your vise. Attach your UTC 70 or Veevus 8/0 thread and evenly coat the entire shank and close both front and rear loops with a thin base of thread.

Step 7   Wind your thread back to the rear of the shank and tie in a clump of Hareline's Black Finn Raccoon Fur. This clump of fur should equal about a marabou plume worth of material that is roughly 3 inches long. If you take your free hand you can evenly disperse the fur around the shank by simply twisting the fur with your fingers.

Step 8   Attach a 3-inch piece of Nuked Green Bean Aqua Veil and evenly wrap the chenille toward the point on the shank where the two wires form to make the eye. Secure the chenille with several thread wraps.

Step 9   Tie in a second clump of Hareline's Black Finn Raccoon Fur. This clump of fur should equal about a marabou plume worth of material that is roughly 3 inches long. If you take your free hand you can evenly disperse the fur around the shank by simply twisting the fur with your fingers.

Step 10   Palmer a nice rear collar with a Chartreuse guinea feather, by tying the feather in by the tip so that the curve of the feather is facing down over top of the fly. This should look like an upside-down boat. Slowly wind the guinea toward the eye while pulling back on the feather fibers so they don't become tangled in each wrap. I typically wrap around the shank four times and tie off, but you can go thicker by adding a couple extra wraps.

Step 11   Attach a set of four Large Blue Senyodelic bead chain eyes to the bottom of the shank where the front two wires meet to form the shank eye and secure with several figure-eight thread wraps. You can add a drop of super glue to the middle of the eyes for added strength. Dub your thread with a sparse amount of Pink Lady Fusion Dubbing and make a figure-eight wrap around the bead chain eyes.

Step 12   To create the veil, take a pinch of chartreuse laser dub and emerald green ice dubbing, place the materials together and pull them apart with your fingers several times to blend them together. Take the clump of dubbing and center tie it over and under the bead chain eyes. Fold the rest of the material over and build a thread head.

23

THE STRAY DOG

This simplified variant of the Temple Dog has always been a favorite among the students in my fly tying classes over the years. This is mainly due to the fact that this fly can be created with six materials and in six steps or less, all while still retaining its intended swim action and the appeal of the original. The main reason I started tying this pattern was to provide a functional and quick pattern that a new tier/angler could use to build their confidence. Those who were looking to start fishing a swung fly could fill a box effectively with one or two patterns and in a multitude of colors. This style is easy to change in size, which makes it a great choice for those fishing multiple species and want to practice their spey casting on local waterways.

Over the past couple years I've added more and more synthetics to this design to shorten the tying steps. This is the most current update with the addition of the Fusion Dubbing to replace extra hackling in the collar. If you are new to this style of tying and want to get in the game, this is a great fly to get you started in the right direction. If anything this is a version that will fill your box, entice fish, and get you moving forward with tying and creating flies of your own.

Target Species   Migratory and resident trout, Alaskan rainbow and char, Pacific salmon, and Great Lakes/PNW steelhead

Favorite Colors   Black, Orange, White, Blue, Purple, Pink, Olive, Chartreuse, and Brown

THE STRAY DOG MATERIALS

Thread   Rusty Brown UTC 70 or Veevus 8/0 (8V-323)

Shank   25mm Orange Flymen Fishing Company Senyo Steelhead/Salmon Shank (25SA-271)

Loop   Senyo's Intruder Wire or Berkley Original Fused Fireline (THW-11)

Tag   Hareline Dubbin Inc. Copper Flat Diamond Braid (FD-320)

Body   Senyo Peanut Brittle Aqua Veil (SA7)

Wing   Hareline Dubbin Inc. Brown Arctic Fox or Heritage Angling Products Brown Silver Fox (AFT-40)

Flash   Pink Flashabou (FLA-6918) and Speckled Copper Flashabou (FLA-6934)

Collar 1   Senyo Crusty Nail Fusion dub (FUS-1)

Collar 2   Hareline Dubbin Inc. Rusty Brown Strung Guinea feather (SGF-323)

Eyes   Jungle cock or Hareline Dubbin Inc. Real Fake Jungle Cock Eyes (FJ-5)

Hook   Partridge, Daiichi, Owner, Gamakatsu size 2–4 Intruder Style (D2557)

THE STRAY DOG TYING INSTRUCTIONS

Step 1   Place an Orange 40mm Senyo Steelhead Shank from Flymen Fishing Company in your vise. Attach your UTC 70 or Veevus 8/0 thread and evenly coat the entire shank and close both front and rear loops with a thin base of thread. Cut off a 4-inch piece of Senyo's Intruder Wire or 30-pound Berkley Fireline and secure it to both sides of the shank with several thread wraps. Take the tag ends through the bottom of the front loop and fold over the top of the shank. Pull tight over the top of the shank and tie down securely with several even thread wraps. Adding glue for strength is optional. Your wire loop should not exceed 2 inches in length.

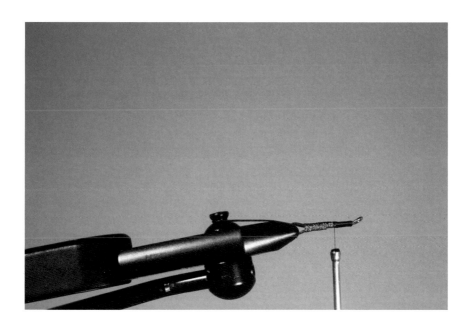

Step 2   Wind your thread back to the rear of the shank and tie in a 2-inch section of the Copper Flat Diamond Braid. Wrap the Braid forward until it covers the section of the shank where the two wires meet and secure with several thread wraps.

Step 3   Cut off a pencil thickness amount of Brown Arctic Fox. Prep the fox by pulling out the short underfur, by holding tightly to the top of the fur and pulling gently from the bottom. Don't go crazy trying to get it all out, as it is good to leave some of it behind. Trim the scissor cut end of the fur to a straight edge one more time and tie the fur wing in reverse where your flat braid ended and wind your thread forward to lock the material in place. Make sure you leave enough room at the eye area of the shank to finish the fly steps to come. Add four to six strands of Pink Flashabou over the wing to finish off this step.

Step 4   Wind your thread back to the point where the copper braid ended, and tie in a 4-inch piece of Senyo's Peanut Brittle Aqua Veil. Wrap the Aqua Veil evenly forward to form the body and underwing of the pattern. Lock in it in as close to the fox fur with several thread wraps and trim off any excess material.

Step 5 Bring your thread to the front of the fox wing, and pull back tightly on the fox and make a few thread wraps right up against the fox. Wetting the fur with water will allow you to stoke the fur backward with ease. Next take a sparse clump of crusty nail fusion dub and center tie it in around the shank just in front of the Arctic Fox. Take a wire brush and firmly comb out fibers to give it a bushy appearance. Top off the wing after the dubbing with five or six strands of Speckled Copper Flashabou.

Step 6 Palmer a nice collar with Hareline Dubbin Inc. Rusty Brown Guinea feather, by tying the feather in by the tip so that the curve of the feather is facing down over top of the fly. This should look like an upside-down boat. Slowly wind the feather toward the eye while pulling back on the feather fibers so they don't become tangled in each wrap. Add a set of Hareline's Real Fake Jungle or Jungle Cock Feather. Build an even thread head and tie off.

BEACH BUM

This is the only fly I really need to fish off the beaches any more. Tying these types of flies are not new as plenty of saltwater anglers have been tying baitfish imitations with similar synthetics and natural materials for many years. For me, the addition of SF Blend really hits all the criteria for a Great Lakes surf fly. SF Blend absorbs no water and becomes virtually transparent with the intended hue when submerged. You can sprinkle in the color of flash you desire and really create a large profile baitfish with very little effort. By adding the new age synthetic dubbings and their color spectra, you can virtually mirror all major forage fish. Forming the fat head profile of the Beach Bum with fox or raccoon gives the fly added movement when the fly is paused on the retrieve. The introduction of realistic eyes such as the Fish Skull Living Eyes have really added to the focal points that trigger predatory fish. I really believe mottling and barring marks are important to finish representing many forage fish. I'm really a fan of UV Barred Predator Wrap because it is subtler than using markers, and imitates that small spotting and speckling seen on a variety of baitfish.

When casting in the Great Lakes surf, your fly size and the distance you may need to cast may not be in agreement. Because the Beach Bum is the illusion of bulk and primarily tied with synthetics, it sheds water and allows you to cast easier. Again I like to tie this pattern on a shank because it gives me just a little bit of weight, but still allows me to easily change to different hook styles such as trebles, stinger, or saltwater hooks.

Target Species   Surf fishing for Great Lakes steelhead, salmon, walleye, and bass

Favorite Color Combos   Olive/Silver, Chartreuse/Pearl, Black/Gold, Blue/Silver, Tan/Pearl, and White/Silver.

BEACH BUM MATERIALS

Shank   Flymen Fishing Company Black 40mm Senyo Steelhead/Salmon Shank (40SA-11)

Thread   UTC 70 or Veevus 8/0 White (8V-377)

Wire   Hareline Dubbin Inc. Senyo Intruder Wire or Berkley Original Fused Fireline (THW-165)

Body   Hareline Dubbin Inc. Flat Silver Diamond Braid (FD-344)

Underwing   Steve Farrar Red SF Blend (FBL-27)

Flash   Silver Lateral Scale (LSC-1701)

Wing   Steve Farrar Aqua Marine SF Blend (FBL-40)

Thorax   Senyo Fishmas Fusion Dub (FUS-5)

Flash   Senyo UV Barred Predator Wrap (BPW-2)

Head   Hareline Dubbin Inc. Gray Arctic Fox or Finn Raccoon Fur (AZ-165)

Eyes   Flymen Fishing Company Fish Skull Living Eyes (4LE-4)

Hook   Partridge, Gamakatsu, or Owner size 2–4 Intruder style hook (D2557)

BEACH BUM TYING INSTRUCTIONS

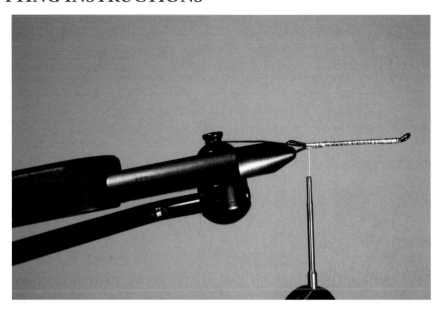

Step 1   Place a Black 40mm Senyo Steelhead Shank from Flymen Fishing Company in your vise. Attach your UTC 70 or Veevus 10/0 thread and evenly coat the entire shank and close both front and rear loops with a thin base of thread. Cut off a 4-inch piece of Senyo's Intruder Wire or 30-pound Berkley Fireline and secure it to both sides of the shank with several thread wraps. Take the tag ends through the bottom of the front loop and fold over the top of the shank. Pull tight over the top of the shank and tie down securely with several even thread wraps. Adding glue for strength is optional. Your wire loop length should not exceed 2 inches in total length.

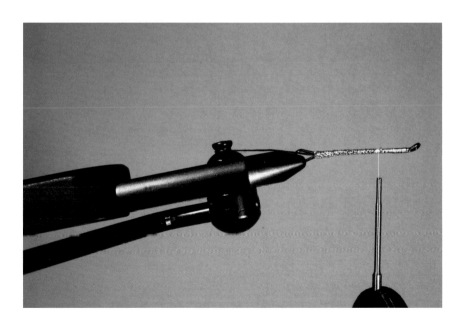

Step 2   Tie in a 4-inch piece of Silver Flat diamond braid and evenly wrap the braid forward, stopping just behind were the two wires of the shank stop to form the eye.

Step 3   Tie in a sparse underwing with red SF Blend around the shank. The fibers should extend to the end of the wire loop.

Step 4   Tie in eight to ten strands of 4-inch long silver lateral scale flashabou. Add a nice wing over the top of the flash with Aqua Marine SF Blend and lock down the material with several thread wraps.

Step 5   Grab a generous Clump of Fishmas Fusion Dub and center tie the dubbing in just in front of the wing. Take and bring your thread to the front and pull the front fibers of the dubbing toward the rear. Use a wire brush and roughly comb out loose fibers and force the material back to blend into the wing.

Step 6   Cut off twelve to fifteen strands of Senyo UV Barred Predator Wrap and tie in over the top of the finished wing and secure.

Step 7   To finish off the head of the fly cut a pencil sized clump of arctic fox or finn raccoon and tie it in around the wing.

Step 8   Add a set of Fish Skull Silver Living Eyes to each side of the head with Loctite gel. *Note:* Crazy Glue is now available with a brush allowing clean and easy application. I rarely whip finish and mainly use just a quick half hitch anymore. The glue as a finish application to the thread is stronger than any knot you can tie.

25

SWAY CRAY

Nearly every Great Lakes tributary or trout river I've had the opportunity to fish from cast to west had some type of crayfish living under its rocks. Color and size is always different depending on where you were, but that is really the least of your problems if you don't have an imitation to carry with you. For a long time I'd over look these freshwater lobsters. Most of the time I would just stick to fishing a sculpin or baitfish imitation because it seemed to make more sense to me as a trout food source. Any time I used to think about a crayfish fly, my brain would conjure up some type of warmwater bass fishing scenario.

The failure to correct my misjudgment would have been a big mistake, and I created the Sway Cray to fill a void in my arsenal. It quickly became a favorite searching pattern on rivers for large brown trout and a favorite springtime fly on the Great Lakes tributaries for steelhead and smallmouth bass.

I may change tactics, from two-handed swinging presentations to a single-handed rod with a light sinking line or tip system. I try more and more often to tie patterns that I can cross over and fish with whatever techniques I choose, based on the river and conditions. This is why you have seen the majority of the flies in this book tied on shanks. I try to complete one box to do the job.

I like to keep the flash to a minimum on this crayfish pattern and resort to more contrasting natural colors. All the materials have different levels of movement and with the addition of the Micro Pulsator Rabbit Strips this fly reacts well when swung across the current, or stripped for an erratic movement. Most of the time I will employ both methods in the same drift.

Target Species   Migratory and resident trout, smallmouth bass, and Great Lakes steelhead

Favorite Colors   Black, Orange, Olive, Tan, and Brown.

SWAY CRAY MATERIALS

Thread   Rusty Brown UTC 70 or Veevus 8/0 (8V-323)

Shank   40mm Orange Flymen Fishing Company Senyo Steelhead/Salmon Shank (40SA-271)

Loop   Senyo's Intruder Wire or Berkley Original Fused Fireline (THW-11)

Tail   Hareline Dubbin Inc. Brown Arctic Fox or Heritage Angling Products Brown Silver Fox (AFT-40)

Claws   Hareline Dubbin Inc. Black Barred Gold Variant Micro Pulsator Rabbit Strips (MPS-7)

Hackle   Hareline Dubbin Inc. Fiery Brown Schlappen Feather (SCHL-114)

Rib   15-pound Fluorocarbon tippet

Body   Senyo Tobacco Fusion dub (FUS-14)

Shellback   Hareline Dubbin Inc. Tan Lady Amherst Center Tail Feather (LAC-369)

Legs   Hareline Dubbin Inc. Rusty Brown Lady Amherst Center Tail Feather (LAC-323)

Collar   Hareline Dubbin Inc. Rusty Brown Strung Guinea Feather (SGF-323)

Hook   Partridge, Daiichi, Owner, Gamakatsu size 2–4 Intruder Style (D2557)

SWAY CRAY TYING INSTRUCTIONS

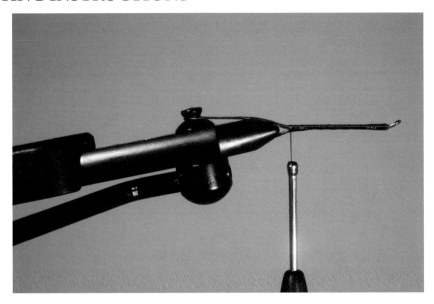

Step 1   Place an Orange 40mm Senyo Steelhead Shank from Flymen Fishing Company in your vise. Attach your UTC 70 or Veevus 8/0 thread and evenly coat the entire shank and close both front and rear loops with a thin base of thread. Cut off a 4-inch piece of Senyo's Intruder Wire or 30-pound Berkley Fireline and secure it to both sides of the shank with several thread wraps. Take the tag ends through the bottom of the front loop and fold over the top of the shank. Pull tight over the top of the shank and tie down securely with several even thread wraps. Adding glue for strength is optional. Your wire loop length should not exceed 2 inches in total length.

Step 2   Take and cut off a pencil sized amount of Brown Arctic Fox. Prep the fox by cutting off the top 2 inches of the fur and securing it around the shank.

Step 3   Cut two pieces of Black Barred Gold Variant Pulsator Strip. Each strip should be roughly 3 inches long, and they should be secured to the shank on each side of the fox hair. These will form the claws of your crayfish.

Step 4   Attach a 6-inch piece of 15-pound fluorocarbon and allow it to hang off the back for later steps. Tie in a fiery brown Schlappen feather by the tip and also allow it to hang off the rear. Add tobacco fusion dubbing to your thread and create an even and compact body along the shank, stopping where the two front wires of the shank form the eye.

Step 5 Take the hanging Schlappen feather and palmer several even wraps forward just as you would do when creating a woolly bugger.

Step 6 Cut off a ¼-inch section of Tan Lady Amherst Center Tail feather and tie it in by the base. Fold the feathers over top of the hackle and dubbing body, so that the tips protrude roughly 1 inch out the back. Take your hanging piece of 15-pound fluorocarbon and rib in between the hackles and evenly over the Amherst tail feathers. It should take six to eight wraps to bring your fluorocarbon to the front and then secure it with several thread wraps.

Step 7   To create the longer legs of the crayfish, rotate your vise and tie in six to eight individual Rusty Brown Lady Amherst Center Tail feathers to the underbelly of the pattern and secure.

Step 8   Palmer a nice collar with Hareline Dubbin Inc. Rusty Brown Guinea feather, by tying the feather in by the tip so that the curve of the feather is facing down over top of the fly. This should look like an upside-down boat. Slowly wind the feather toward the eye while pulling back on the feather fibers so they don't become tangled in each wrap. Trim off any remaining feather and build a nice thread head.

26

THE WILLEN MICRO NICKEL

The micro nickel came to be by simply downsizing an existing musky pattern. The real story behind this fly starts on the Chippewa River in northern Wisconsin. In 2012, I started trying to tweak a pattern that was very successful. I wanted to achieve just a little more depth with the fly. But not so much to snag the bottom or structure with regularity. So instead of adding lead, I used lighter-weight aluminum sea eyes and encased them in bucktail hair. The result was just what I wanted. The fly came to the boat just a little deeper and had this head bobbing action that looked very much like a struggling meal. The first day using this "double nickel," Brian Porter and I landed two mid 40-inch musky on Lake Namekagon. That's when I thought, "ok this will work." I continued to use the fly with a lot of success for musky, slightly tweaking the bulk of the pattern until I found what I thought to be the perfect combination of weight and hair.

Then it occurred to me that this fly could also successfully target bass, trout, pike, walleye, and pretty much anything that eats baitfish, if I just reduced the size of the pattern to about one quarter of its original size. I started messing around with sizes and getting some fish. All was good, "but what about targeting trout?" Since I don't have the big streamer water for trout where I guide, nor really the time to pursue trophy trout with this pattern, I ended up tying a bunch and sending them to Pennsylvania to well-known trout guide Lance Wilt. As it turned out, they worked great for Lance and his clients. So much so, he tried ordering ten dozen shortly after the first batch arrived. Depending on hook size and material bulk, this streamer can serve as a universal pattern for minnow/sucker eating fish. Thus the Willen Micro Nickel earned its place as a staple streamer for myself and a few other trout guides across the U.S.

Target Species   Resident trout, pike, walleye, and smallmouth bass

Favorite Color Combinations   White, Black, Rust, Chartreuse, Olive, Tan, Yellow, Brown

THE WILLEN MICRO NICKEL MATERIALS

Rear Hook   Gamakatsu B-10S size 2

Thread   Veevus 150 GSP (150G-11)

Shoulder   Hareline Dubbin Inc. Yellow Northern Bucktail (NB-383)

Tail   Hareline Dubbin Inc. Yellow Strung Saddle Hackle (SCSD-383)

Flash   Hedron Inc. Holographic Gold Flashabou (HFL-6992)

Shoulder 2   Hareline Dubbin Inc. White Northern Bucktail (NB-377)

Overwing   Hareline Dubbin Inc. Yellow Strung Saddle Hackle (SCSD-383)

Collar 1   Hareline Dubbin Inc. White Northern Bucktail (NB-377)

Collar 2   Hareline Dubbin Inc. Yellow Northern Bucktail (NB-383)

Front Hook   Gamakatsu B-10S Size 1

Connection   Hareline Dubbin Inc. Trailer Hook Wire (THW-165)

Beads   6mm Green and Gold Pro Eye

Shoulder 1   Hareline Dubbin Inc. Olive Northern Bucktail (NB-263)

Shoulder 2   Hareline Dubbin Inc. Olive Northern Bucktail (NB-263)

Flash   Peacock Crystal Flash (KF-17)

Collar   Hareline Dubbin Inc. Yellow Northern Bucktail (NB-383)

Wing   Hareline Dubbin Inc. Yellow Strung Saddle Hackle (SCSD-383)

Barbell   Hareline Dubbin Inc. Large Black Nickel Sunken Barbell Eyes (SKL-11)

Head   Hareline Dubbin Inc. Premo Deer Hair Strips Golden Brown (PDH-157)

Head 2   Hareline Dubbin Inc. Premo Deer Hair Strips Dark Brown (PDH-87)

Eyes   5/16 Super Pearl 3D Adhesive Eyes (OP5-367)

THE WILLEN MICRO NICKEL TYING INSTRUCTIONS

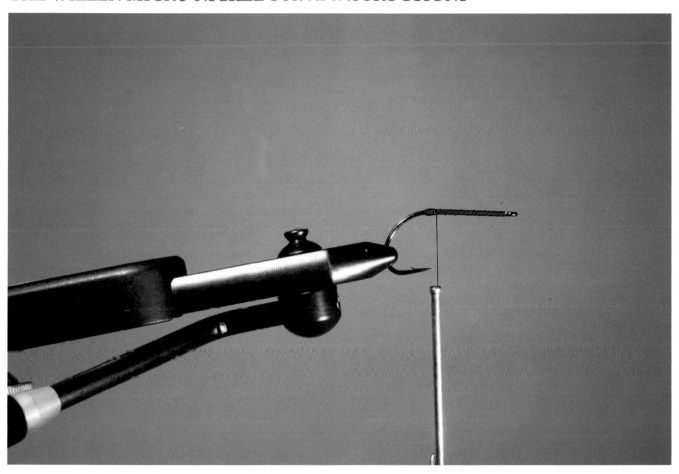

Step 1   Evenly coat the rear Gamakatsu B-10s size 2 hook with Veevus 150 GSP thread.

Step 2   Tie in a clump of Hareline Dubbin Inc. Yellow Northern Bucktail onto the hook shank beginning your tie in point just around the point of the hook. Tie a few turns back to secure and then forward, leave some trim of bucktail for shoulder flare.

Step 3   Take a pinch of Hedron Inc. Holographic Gold Flashabou, and secure just in front of the first clump of bucktail. The flashabou will be used to construct part of the tail, so it should reach back past the end of the hook about 3–4 inches in length.

Step 4   At roughly the same tie-in point as the flashabou, tie in two Hareline Dubbin Inc. Yellow Strung Saddle Hackles, one on each side of the hook shank. Advance your thread forward over the stems to secure. The saddle hackle tips should reach back beyond the hook about 3–4 inches.

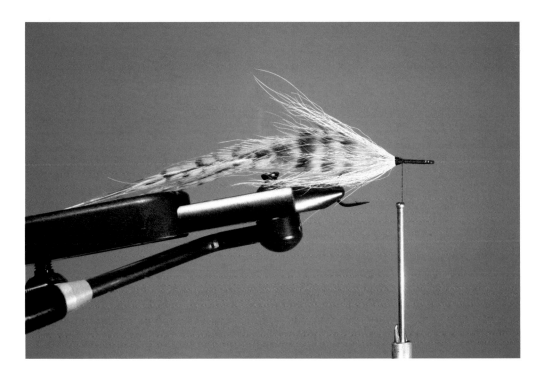

Step 5   Taking about the same amount of bucktail that you used for the tail, reverse-tie another clump of bucktail, this time with minimal flare. Fold the bucktail back over itself so the tips are facing the rear of the hook and secure. Reverse-tie a pinch of flashabou in a similar manner as the bucktail.

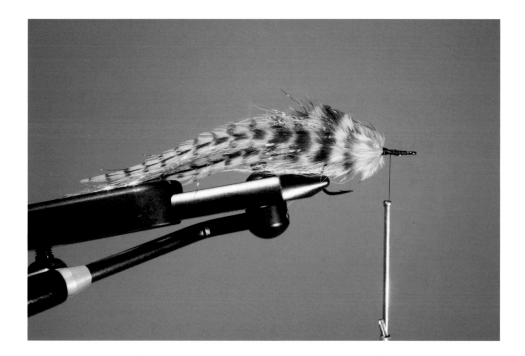

Step 6   For an overwing, tie in two saddle hackles, one on each side of the shank, slightly farther along the hook shank than previous saddle hackles. The tips of the saddle hackles should reach beyond the rear of the hook to the same length. This will leave a little more webbing exposed on these two saddles, but that is ok.

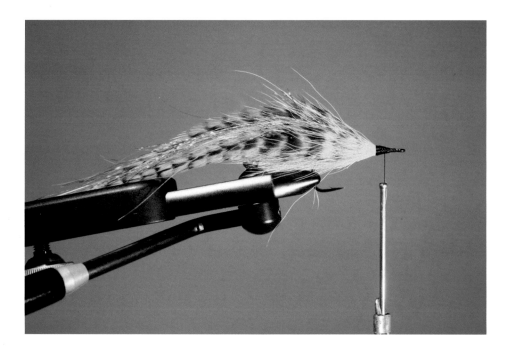

Step 7   Reverse-tie another clump of yellow bucktail, slightly larger flare than first clump. Fold the bucktail back over itself again, similar to the previous clump. Reverse-tie another pinch of flashabou, cut in half lengths for body flash, not to extend to the tail. Complete the rear hook with one more clump of reverse-tied white bucktail. Make this final clump with shorter fibers, but your "thickest" clump having the most flare.

Step 8 Secure and cover the bucktail. Whip finish and super glue.

Step 9 For the connection, take a 4-inch piece of Hareline Dubbin Inc. Trailer Hook wire with two 6mm Green and Gold Pro Eye beads. Thread the wire first through the eye of the rear hook, then add the two beads over the wire, so that both ends of the wire thread through the beads and can be tied securely to the front hook. Remove the rear hook from the vise and replace with the front hook, a Gamakatsu B-10s size 1 hook. Tie in the connection wire tips on top of the front hook shank and coat with super glue.

Step 10   Cover the wire connection and beads, by tying in a clump of Hareline Dubbin Inc. Olive Northern Bucktail onto the hook shank, beginning your tie-in point just around the point of the hook. Tie a few turns back to secure and then forward, leave some trim of bucktail for shoulder flare.

Step 11   Reverse-tie another clump of Hareline Dubbin Inc. Olive Northern Bucktail. This clump should be slightly larger flare than the last step on the rear hook, so as to keep a nice taper. Fold the bucktail back over itself so the tips are facing the rear of the hook and secure.

Step 12 Reverse-tie a pinch of Peacock Crystal Flash in a similar manner as the bucktail to extend back over the connection point, but not longer than the bucktail fibers.

Step 13 Reverse-tie more Hareline Dubbin Inc. Yellow Northern Bucktail, continuing to gain bulk as you move toward the head of the fly.

Step 14   Form the wing, by tying in two Hareline Dubbin Inc. Yellow Strung Saddle Hackles, one on each side of the hook.

Step 15   Tie in Hareline Dubbin Inc. Large Black Nickel Sunken Barbell Eyes on the bottom of the shank leaving ample space for spinning hair in front of eyes, but well enough behind the hook eye.

Step 16   To form the head, cut some long spin-able Hareline Dubbin Inc. Premo Deer Hair in Golden Brown. With the fibers pointed back, tie in behind the eyes and spin the ends around the eyes. Tying through the fibers and advancing the thread wraps through the fibers to lock them in and angle them forward.

Step 17   Use body hair or short spin-able fibers from the bottom of a bucktail. Trim the pointed ends. Spin the deer hair in front of the eyes pushing fibers back (stacking) to fill the gap between the eyes making the head of the fly look like one solid unit. Whip finish and super glue.

Step 18   Trim the head to a rounded face/head of the fly. Glue 5/16 Super Pearl 3D Adhesive Eyes into your seas eyes recessed eye holders.

THE SCHULTZY SWINGIN' D

Growing up and fishing Michigan has given me a back-stage pass to some of the best streamer anglers in the game. I've been fortunate to converse, fish and compare notes with some of the most innovative streamer tiers in our sport. Guys like Mark Sedotti, Tommy Lynch and Russ Maddin have helped shape the way I approach fly design beyond the nose-weighted streamer.

My original working name for this fly was the Meat Whip, but the Swingin' D evolved shortly thereafter. This fly is heavily influenced by

Tommy Lynch's Drunk and Disorderly series, optimized for the smallmouth bass rivers of Michigan. It suspends, it's erratic, and it moves in all directions: If it looks like a wounded fish, it gets eaten like a wounded fish!

I started working with foam heads in the summer of 2011. At first, I used a reversed-foam popper head with a wedge shape, but I quickly found several issues with the design. The first problem was buoyancy, as the original heads were difficult to fish beyond 2 feet. The second problem I discovered was too much line twisting. The block wedge head would sometimes roll, twisting the fly line and making it difficult for the angler to continually cast without having to break and untwist their fly line.

In the winter 2012, I discovered Rainy's Foam Diver Heads. This instantly made the fly easier to fish. Keeping the majority of the weight on the front hook, in combination with a Dahlberg Diver–shaped head allowed the fly to suspend. The foam head is designed to push water over the fly, which drives the action. Picture an empty tractor-trailer on an icy road, struggling to maintain control.

The Swingin' D fishes best with a sharp, straight strip and pause—there's no need for extra rod movement. Just keep the tip to the water and mix up your retrieve. Fishing down and across moving water while holding the fly in the sweet spot has proven to be the best. Another bonus of the Swingin' D is that it is durable and easy to tie. The rattles, flash, and motion translate into fish!

I prefer light-colored versions for this fly, such as white, chartreuse, or yellow. Being able to see the fly why you're working it through the water is a huge advantage. Like most swim-bait patterns, the Swingin' D fishes best on a full intermediate line, with a 4–6 foot tapered leader from a 25-pound butt section down to a 16-pound tippet.

Target Species   Smallmouth bass, pike, and trout

Favorite Color Combinations   Gray, White, Chartreuse, Olive, Clown (Multi Colored)

THE SCHULTZY SWINGIN' D MATERIALS

Rear Hook   Gamakatsu B-10S size 4

Thread   Veevus 6/0 Flo. Yellow Chartreuse (6V-143)

Tail   Hareline Dubbin Inc. Gray Strung Saddle Hackle (SCSD-165)

Flash   Pearl Lateral Scale (LSC-1703)

Body Hackle   Hareline Dubbin Inc. Senyo's UV Barred Predator Wrap (BPW-2)

Collar   Hareline Dubbin Inc. White Rabbit Zonker Strip (MRS-377)

Wing   Hareline Dubbin Inc. Natural Mallard Flank Feather (BMF-242)

Front Hook   Gamakatsu Worm (Round Bend) size 2/0

Connection   Hareline Dubbin Inc. Trailer Hook Wire (THW-165)

Beads   3 Pro Eye Silver 6mm

Flash   Pearl Lateral Scale (LSC-1703)

Rear Collar   Hareline Dubbin Inc. White Rabbit Zonker Strip (MRS-377)

Body   Hareline Dubbin Inc. Senyo's UV Barred Predator Wrap (BPW-2)

Rattle   Glass 5mm (RAT-5) Marabou wrapped tip first (two to four wraps max).

Collar   Hareline Dubbin Inc. White Marabou Blood Quill (MSBQ-377)

Wing   Hareline Dubbin Inc. Grizzly hackle (GRIZM-247)

Throat   Hareline Dubbin Inc. UV Pink Polar Chenille (PCUV-188)

Head   Rainy's Small White Foam Diver Head

Tying Tips   Use Loctite Gel Super Glue on the throat before sliding the head over. Keep the rear hook light; for a tuned action, keep it sparse with the majority of the weight up front.

THE SCHULTZY SWINGIN' D TYING INSTRUCTIONS

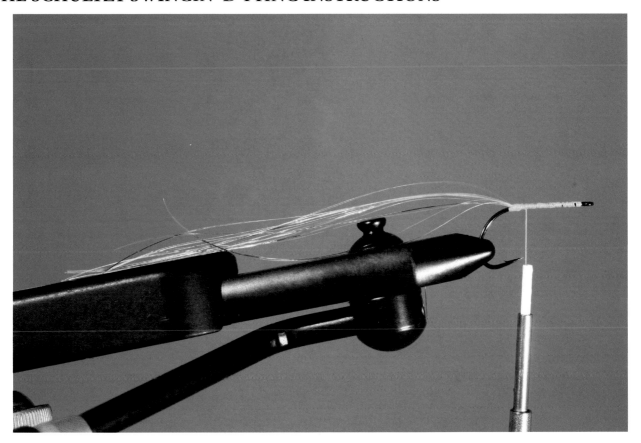

Step 1   Tie the rear hook first by coating a Gamakatsu B-10s size 4 hook with an even layer of Veevus 6/0 Flo Yellow Chartreuse thread. Stop your thread just before the bend of the hook and tie in about 2–3 inch lengths of some Pearl Lateral Scale Flash.

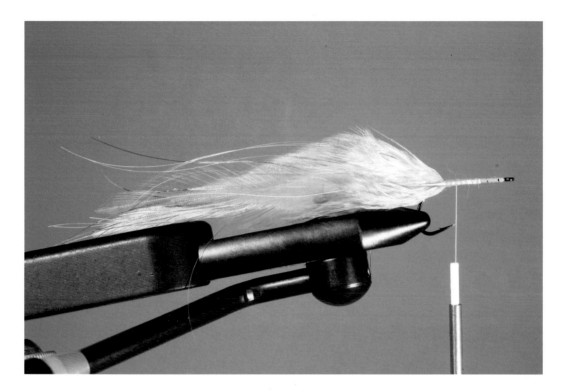

Step 2 Tie one Hareline Dubbin Inc. Gray Strung Saddle Hackle on each side of the hook to form the tail. Tie so that the convex sides face each other. Your saddles should stretch back off the rear of the hook to give you a 3–4 inch tail.

Step 3 For the rear body, tie in Hareline Dubbin Inc. Senyo's UV Barred Predator Wrap trimmed and stroked back towards the rear of the fly to evenly spread the Predator Wrap.

Step 4   Follow with Hareline Dubbin Inc. White Rabbit Zonker Strip clipped off the hide and spun in a dubbing loop. Wet your fingers and stroke the dubbed rabbit towards the rear of the fly.

Step 5   Tie in a single Hareline Dubbin Inc. Natural Mallard Flank Feather or Silver Pheasant feather as your overwing. Tie in at the point where you tied off your rabbit. This will complete the rear hook.

Step 6   Prepare the connection by using a 4-inch piece of Hareline Dubbin Inc. Trailer Hook Wire with three Pro Eye Silver 6mm beads. The wire should first thread through the eye of the rear hook, then slip the beads over both end of the wire before removing from the vise. Add the front hook to the vise. For the front hook, use a Gamakatsu Worm (Round Bend) size 2/0 hook and the same thread as the rear. Secure the wire connection to the front hook by laying both ends of the wire along the shank of the front hook and tying down. Allow just a teardrop-sized loop between the first bead and the rear hook eye: this will prevent the hooks from fowling up.

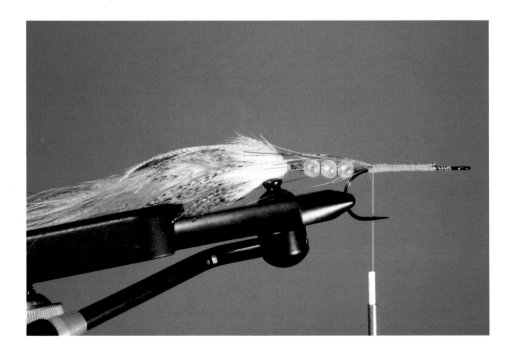

Step 7   After securing the connection, tie in some Pearl Lateral Scale Flash at the rear of the front hook. Make it long enough to cover the connection wire.

Step 8   Tie in a Hareline Dubbin Inc. White Rabbit Zonker Strip wrapped two or three times. Stroke the rabbit back as your wrap so that all the rabbit hair flows towards the rear of the hook. Tie off and trim.

Step 9   Tie in Senyo's Predator Wrap trimmed, so that the long fibers are roughly 1–1½ inches in length. Tie in a large Glass 5mm rattle. Make sure the rattle is good and secure and finish with the thread just past the rattle on the hook shank.

Step 10   Palmer the Predator Wrap over the rattle. Stroke the Predator Wrap evenly as you palmer it so as not to over dress in one spot. Tie off the Predator Wrap.

Step 11   Tie in a Hareline Dubbin Inc. White Marabou Blood Quill feather wrapped tip first. Make two to four wraps max. Wet your fingers and pull the Marabou back towards the rear of the hook as you wrap around the shank to ensure a nice even veil of Marabou.

Step 12   Tie in one Hareline Dubbin Inc. Grizzly hackle feather on each side of the hook shank to form some lateral lines.

Step 13   Form a throat by tying Hareline Dubbin Inc. UV Pink Polar Chenille wrapped to the eye of the hook. Stroke the fibers with your finger towards the rear of the hook as your wrap.

Step 14   Add a drop of Loctite glue behind the eye of the hook and slide on the Rainy's Foam Diver Head in small or medium, so that the flat side is facing down. Slide back far enough so that the eye of the hook is exposed at the end of the diver head. Before this step, consider sliding the diver head on once without the Loctite to measure that you have left yourself enough room.

28

LYNCH MINI-D

W hen I was young there was a thick, black line between conventional tactics and whatever fly-fishing applications were considered back then when the sport wasn't as well-known or popular as it is today. Things are very different today. We see lure-like flies that swim, maneuver, and undulate thanks to all the new materials in our quiver each time we sit down to tie up the next bit of goodness. These newer synthetic replacements or enhancements to our fly tying vise are making it easier for us to bridge the gap between lures that swim, shake, and sound off ... *and flies that would do the same*. Many swing fishermen would never have considered throwing a large straight Flashabou pattern at a steelhead, thinking it maybe too offensive. But that is like saying that a Chrome & Chartreuse Hot & Tot won't work. Growing up fishing both terminal and fly presentations, I had a really good sense of trigger watching all those crank baits come through the water, and also what it took to make a fish chase; not only when he was on the bite and feeding, but also when he wasn't. I think anglers spend too much time changing flies instead of changing presentation angles, or just giving yourself an attitude adjustment, and fishing a fly better as if a fish has already taken notice. My best clients don't change flies often, they simply fish the fly better and with a confidence that catches more than any fly in my box. And I have some dandies! Having flies with bling and rattle, chuck and jive—thanks to all the materials we are allowed to experiment with these days—keeps my clients glued to the pattern and presentation, which in turn leads to confidence, just like watching a Rapala come through the water ... it just looks like it's gonna get killed!

With all the cool materials, enhancements in head curing, rattles, et cetera, it kind of silly to think we are just tying wooly buggers these days. Anglers use our flies on conventional gear, they swim and last as long as some of the lures. We tie now to make bugs that have three to five recovery maneuvers to our one strip, this instead of just jigging a wide array of different material and color behind the same theme of a lead head that has at best, Mr. Twister–like qualities. Lures catch more fish because they simply cater to more of the fish's instinctual responses, by not only looking like a fish, but then sounding like one as well. Bait caters to all four senses and typically goes down the hatch accordingly, but fishing some of today's flies against some of the tried-and-true lures of the past may surprise many of you who just assume that fishing a fly is inferior to any type of swim or jigging artificial. Synthetics have allowed fly fisherman to bridge that gap between what makes a Rapala so much better than a wooly bugger, or why a flashy mess of BOU out fishes traditional steelhead spey flies of years past. The bottom line is that the whole game has changed with the introduction of these cutting-edge fly/lure materials. And there will always be reasons to fish a traditional dry fly or swinging a soft hackle or even spey fly, but with the modern-day twist on a lot of traditional materials, you can likely tie patterns easier with synthetics that are more effective and durable.

Target Species   Great Lakes steelhead, brown trout, and smallmouth bass

Favorite Color Combinations   Tan, White, Chartreuse, Black, Yellow, Orange, Olive, Fire Tiger

LYNCH MINI-D MATERIALS

Thread   Brown UTC 140 or Veevus 6/0 (6V-323)

Rear Hook   Gamakatsu B-10S size 4

Flash   Hedron Inc. Holographic Fire Tiger Flashabou (HFL-3285)

Body   Hareline Dubbin Inc. Hot Orange UV Polar Chenille (PCUV-187)

Collar   Hareline Dubbin Inc. Black Barred Chartreuse Rabbit Strip (BRS-54)

Wing   Hareline Dubbin Inc. Orange Mallard Flank Feather (MF-271)

Wire   Hareline Dubbin Inc. Trailer Hook Wire (THW-165)

Beads   6mm copper Pro Eye bead

Front Hook   Daiichi 4x long Streamer Hook size 6 (DX220-6)

Rattle   5mm Glass (RAT-5)

Head   Hareline Dubbin Inc. Chartreuse Premo Deer Hair Strip (PDH-263)

Head 2   Hareline Dubbin Inc. Orange Premo Deer Hair Strip (PDH-271)

Head 3   Hareline Dubbin Inc. Chartreuse Premo Deer Hair Strip (PDH-263)

Head 4   Hareline Dubbin Inc. Orange Premo Deer Hair Strip (PDH-271)

Eyes   Super Pearl 3/8 3D Adhesive Eyes (OP6-367)

Epoxy   Clear Cure Goo Hydro or Loon Outdoors Flow (LN100)

Tying Tips   Use Loctite Gel Super Glue for securing eyes, followed by a coat of Loon Thin Squeeze for durability & dive. Comb out the underfur before stacking your deer hair. Use a hair stacker and packer when tying the head! Pack'em TIGHT. Use scissors and a high quality Wilkerson Swords razor blade when slimping the head.

LYNCH MINI-D TYING INSTRUCTIONS

Step 1   Thread an even coat of Brown UTC 140 or Veevus 6/0 over a Gamakatsu B-10s size 4 hook and end with the thread wraps at the rear of the hook. Tie in a pinch of Hedron Inc. Holographic Fire Tiger Flashabou for the tail. Flash should extend about twice the length of hook.

Step 2 Tie in about 5 inches of Hareline Dubbin Inc. Hot Orange UV Polar Chenille. Wrap the chenille forward toward the eye of the hook. As your wrap, stroke the fibers back so they are evenly distributed around the hook and all facing toward the bend. Tie in.

Step 3 Wrap a piece of Hareline Dubbin Inc. Black Barred Chartreuse Rabbit Strip to complete the body of the rear hook.

Step 4 Cover the rear hook with a single Hareline Dubbin Inc. Orange Mallard Flank Feather. The feather can extend beyond the bend of the hook. Whip finish to complete the rear hook.

Step 5 Create a connection of Hareline Dubbin Inc. Trailer Hook Wire and 6mm copper Pro Eye bead for connecting the front hook to the rear hook. You can use about 4 inches of wire and one 6mm bead. For the connection, pass the wire through the eye of the rear hook dividing the wire into two equal lengths. Pass the bead over both pieces of wire, leaving a small teardrop in front of the rear hook. Remove the rear hook from the vise. Place the front hook, Daiichi 4x long Streamer Hook size 6 in your vise. Tie the wire connector to the rear of your front hook at a point just beyond the bend. Wrap forward to secure the wire to the hook. Be careful to keep the rear hook in line with the front hook. You can make adjustments to the wire position and length after your first two turns of thread. Tie in the rest of the wire to about the midpoint of the hook, fold back any remaining length of wire to face the rear of the front hook and tie down. This should create a nice cradle for the rattle you will tie in later.

Step 6   Tie in some Hedron Inc. Holographic Fire Tiger Flashabou at the rear of the front hook, just after the bend to cover the connection. The flash should be just long enough to cover the midpoint of the rear hook.

Step 7   Tie in a Hareline Dubbin Inc. Black Barred Chartreuse Rabbit Strip and make three or four wraps for a body.

Step 8   At the point where you finished wrapping the rabbit, tie in the Hareline Dubbin Inc. Hot Orange UV Polar Chenille, but do not start to wrap the chenille, as you will palmer it over the rattle. Tie in the 5mm Glass rattle with wraps that secure the rattle. Advance the thread a few turns past the rattle toward the eye of the hook.

Step 9   Palmer the UV Polar Chenille over the rattle. As you wrap, stroke the fibers back so they are evenly distributed around the rattle and facing towards the bend. Tie off the UV Polar Chenille.

Step 10   Tie in one Hareline Dubbin Inc. Orange Mallard Flank Feather of identical size on either side of the hook at the same point you tied off the Polar Chenille. Make sure the flanks curve in toward the body.

Step 11   Tie in some Holographic Fire Tiger Flashabou so that it runs down the center of the hook towards the rear. Tie the flash in at the same point you tied the mallard flank.

Step 12 Tie in another Black Barred Chartreuse Rabbit Strip, wrapping it three or four times toward the eye.

Step 13 Tie in a collar of Hareline Dubbin Inc. Chartreuse Premo Deer Hair.

Step 14   Tie in about three separate "pencils" worth of alternating Chartreuse Premo Deer Hair Strip and Orange Premo Deer Hair.

Step 15   Trim the deer hair to form a nice head.

Step 16 Using Loctite, glue Super Pearl 3/8 3D Adhesive Eyes to both sides of the head. Coat the head and around the eyes with Clear Cure Goo Hydro or Loon Outdoors Flow.

29

Schultz's Chicken Changer (CC) Hybrid

Keeled and Feathered...
I first met Mark Sedotti at Bueter's Fly Shop in the fall of 2004. Later that night I had the chance to watch him tie the Slammer and Kickin' Chick'n. His concepts were eye-opening, since he designed his flies to have "built-in" action that would behave like the real thing. It was a cutting-edge concept. Some of these flies would dart to one side and some in the up and down direction, while others moved in random directions.

He spoke of flies designed to spiral on the drop, or flip suddenly when stripped, flipping back to its original "straight up" position when tension eased. I had seen similar behavior out of some plastic baits, but nothing like this with flies.

Ten plus years have passed and during that time, the choices of fly tying materials and hook styles have grown immensely, allowing for even greater manipulation of fly movement without having to add traditional styles of weight. As a guide, you want a fly to swim with a basic strip for your clients, so finding the right combination of materials that gives the pattern Sedotti's concept of "built-in" movement is key.

The CC (Chick'n Changer) Hybrid utilizes a fairly new and growing concept. I like to tie it similar to Sedotti's Kickin' Chick'n, but with a modern twist! I started incorporating Flymen Fish Spines used for the popular Chocklett Game Changer–style flies, in combination with a wrapped and stacked keel. The swim "living fly" movement it achieves is incredible. Combining the Fish Spine with a keel gives you a universal baitfish pattern that casts like a dart and swims like a fish. I prefer to fish this pattern on an intermediate or sinking line with a 4–6 foot tapered leader with a broken cadence retrieve.

Target Species   Smallmouth bass, pike, and trout

Favorite Color Combinations   Gray, White, Chartreuse, Olive, Clown (Multi Colored)

SCHULTZ'S CHICKEN CHANGER HYBRID MATERIALS

Thread   Chartreuse UTC 140 or Veevus 6/0 (6V-143)

Rear shank   Flymen Fishing Company 10mm articulated Fish Spine (10FS)

Flash   Pearl Lateral Scale Flashabou (LSC-1703)

Tail   Hareline Dubbin Inc. White Saddle Hackle Tips (SCSD-377)

Collar   Hareline Dubbin Inc. White Hen Feathers (1MHN-72)

Shank 2   Flymen Fishing Company 15mm articulated Fish Spine (15FS)

Body   Hareline Dubbin Inc. White Hen Feathers (1MHN-72)

Collar   Hareline Dubbin Inc. Grizzly Soft Hackle Feather (GS-247)

Shank 3   Flymen Fishing Company 20mm articulated Fish Spine (20FS)

Body   Hareline Dubbin Inc. White Hen Feathers (1MHN-72)

Collar   Hareline Dubbin Inc. Grizzly Soft Hackle Feather (GS-247)

Wire   Hareline Dubbin Inc. Trailer Hook Wire (THW-165)

Keel Weight   .025 Spooled Lead Wire (L-25)

Front Hook   Gamakatsu Worm (Round Bend) size 2/0

Flash   Pearl Lateral Scale Flashabou (LSC-1703)

Hackle   Hareline Dubbin Inc. White Schlappen Feather (SCHL-377)

Rear Collar   Hareline Dubbin Inc. Grizzly Soft Hackle Feather (GS-247)

Body   Hareline Dubbin Inc. X Large Pearl Cactus Chenille (XCH)

Wing   Hareline Dubbin Inc. White Northern Bucktail (NB-377)

Gills   Hareline Dubbin Inc. Red Ice Dub (ICE-300)

Flash   Senyo's UV Barred Predator Wrap (BPW-2)

Collar   Hareline Dubbin Inc. Grizzly Saddle Feather (1MHS-176)

Head   Marc Petitjean's Magic Head (PMR3)

Eyes   Clear Cure 3mm Peacock Adhesive Eyes (CA3-3

SCHULTZ'S CHICKEN CHANGER HYBRID TYING INSTRUCTIONS

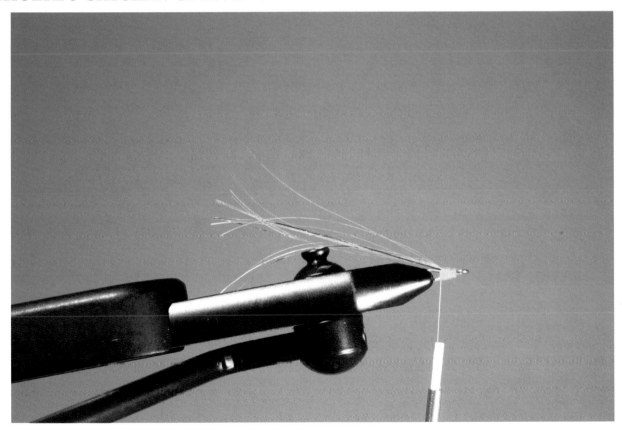

Step 1   For the tail, use a Flymen Fishing Company 10mm articulated Fish Spine shank and Chartreuse UTC 140 or Veevus 6/0 thread. Tie in some Pearl Lateral Scale Flashabou.

Step 2   Tin in four Hareline Dubbin Inc. White Saddle Hackle Tips.

Step 3   To complete the tail, wrap Hareline Dubbin Inc. White Hen Feathers shank. Whip finish.

Step 4 Connect the tail shank to a Flymen Fishing Company 15mm articulated Fish Spine shank. Place the second shank in your vise. Secure the connection by wrapping evenly over the front and back connection links.

Step 5 Tie in and wrap Hareline Dubbin Inc. White Hen Feathers.

Step 6   Tie in a collar of wrapped Hareline Dubbin Inc. Grizzly Soft Hackle Feather.

Step 7   Connect the second shank to a Flymen Fishing Company 20mm articulated Fish Spine. Place the body shank in your vise. Secure the connection by wrapping evenly over the front and back connection links.

Step 8   Tie in and wrap Hareline Dubbin Inc. White Hen Feathers, followed by a collar of wrapped Hareline Dubbin Inc. Grizzly Soft Hackle Feather. Remove from vise.

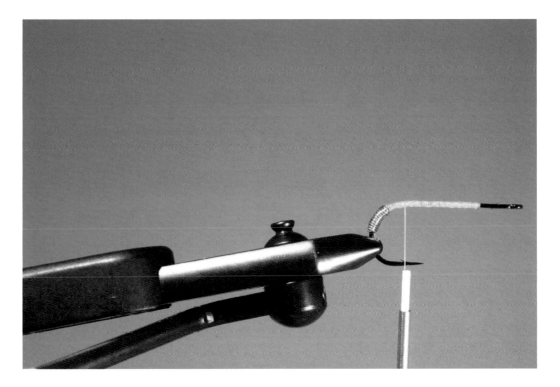

Step 9   Tie a keel .024 lead wire wrapped evenly six to eight times around the bend of a Gamakatsu Worm (Round Bend) size 2/0 hook. Cover with Clear Cure Goo.

Step 10   For the connection from the body shank to the Gamakatsu Worm (Round Bend) size 2/0 hook, use Hareline Dubbin Inc. Trailer Hook Wire or monofilament. Thread the wire through the body shank and tie securely to the hook shank.

Step 11   For the cover, tie in a clump of Pearl Lateral Scale Flashabou so that it extends slightly over the body shank.

Step 12   Form the front body using a Hareline Dubbin Inc. White Schlappen Feather.

Step 13   Follow with Hareline Dubbin Inc. Grizzly Soft Hackle Feather, wrapped to form a rear collar.

Step 14   Tie in some Hareline Dubbin Inc. X Large Pearl Cactus Chenille, wrapped four times around the shank, stroke the fibers towards the rear of the hook to get a nice even flow.

Step 15   Tie in a small pinch of Hareline Dubbin Inc. White Northern Bucktail, just after wrapping the chenille.

Step 16   To form the gills, tie in a few wraps of Hareline Dubbin Inc. Red Ice Dub, stroke the fibers towards the rear of the hook to get a nice even flow.

Step 17   Add some flash with a few wraps of trimmed Senyo's UV Barred Predator Wrap. Trim the tips down to about 1–1½ inches in length. Make two to three careful wraps, separating the fibers as you wrap so they are even around the hook.

Step 18   Tie in a collar of Hareline Dubbin Inc. Grizzly Saddle Feather. Leave about ⅛ inch behind the eye of the hook to tie in the Magic Head.

Step 19   Tie in a Marc Petitjean's Magic Head. You will have to slip the thin tube section over the eye of the hook. Secure with a few wraps of thread over plastic tube. The cone of the tube should not be folded back over the hook yet. It should still be open and facing away from the eye. Glue in using Clear Cure, a pair of 5mm Peacock Adhesive Eyes on the side of the wrapped Grizzly Saddle Feather. You might consider letting this sit for a short period of time before folding the Magic Head back over the eyes. The glue from Clear Cure can cause the Magic Head to "fog" while still drying. Fold the cone of the Magic Head back over the eyes, exposing the hook eye.

30

SCHMIDT'S RED ROCKET

When I hit the river to fish the way that I want to fish, it generally means I am headed to throw streamers at whatever is the day's aggressive meat-eating target species. In my home waters around Ohio, that mostly means that I will be chasing smallmouth or trout. The water that I fish tends to have faster riffle sections separating long and very slow-moving pools, which means that I spend more time than I want changing out streamer patterns to get maximum movement in those varied water conditions. That gave me with the challenge to create an articulated streamer that would have both great movement and profile regardless of water speed. It was a puzzle that took a few attempts, but the resulting combination of a few natural materials along with some synthetics allowed me to create the Red Rocket.

I designed the Red Rocket to be around 5 inches in length and fished on a sinking line to get to the desired depth. At that size, it is small enough so casting is no problem for the average fly fisherman but large enough to represent a meal worthy of a fish moving to intercept it. The Red Rocket utilizes a thick head of Senyo Laser Dub to maintain a wider and taller profile in faster-moving water or during an aggressive strip retrieve. That wider head also pushes a lot of water that comes back together on the back of the fly, giving the tail a very swimmy motion in the water. In slower water the spun marabou over palmered schlappen wiggles enticingly at even the slightest hint of current or movement. By using two different-colored feathers on the rear hook, the fly takes on a more naturally-mottled appearance in the water. I have found that the fly does fish best when retrieved with short and abrupt jerk strips, which speed up the fly before coming to a pause and sharp turn off to the side. More often than not, fish will hammer the fly on that pause or at the first hint that the fly is about to speed back up.

Target Species   Brown trout and bass

Favorite Color Combinations   White, Black, Rust, Chartreuse, Olive, Tan, Yellow, Brown

SCHMIDT'S RED ROCKET MATERIALS

Thread   Black UTC 140 or Veevus 6/0 (6V-11)

Rear Hook   Gamakatsu B-10S size 2

Flash   Hedron Inc. Holographic Gold Flashabou (HFL-6992)

Tail   Hareline Dubbin Inc. Tan Rabbit Zonker Strip (RS-43)

Body   Hareline Dubbin Inc. Large Root Beer Cactus Chenille (CCL-320)

Hackle   Hareline Dubbin Inc. Yellow Schlappen Feather (SCHL-383)

Collar   Hareline Dubbin Inc. Tan Marabou Blood Quill (MSBQ-369)

Rubber Legs   Hareline Dubbin Inc. Speckled Pumpkin Crazy Legs (BL-279)

Wire   Hareline Dubbin Inc. Trailer Hook Wire (THW-165)

Beads   3mm Red Glass beads

Front Hook   Gamakatsu B-10S size 1

Flash   Hedron Inc. Holographic Gold Flashabou (HFL-6992)

Body   Hareline Dubbin Inc. Large Root Beer Cactus Chenille (CCL-320)

Hackle   Hareline Dubbin Inc. Yellow Schlappen Feather (SCHL-383)

Collar   Hareline Dubbin Inc. Tan Marabou Blood Quill (MSBQ-369)

Rubber Legs   Hareline Dubbin Inc. Speckled Pumpkin Crazy Legs (BL-279)

Gills   Hareline Dubbin Inc. Natural Grizzly Mini Marabou (GRIZM247)

Throat   Senyo's Pink Lady Fusion Dub (FUS-10)

Head   Senyo's Tan Laser Dub (SL-369)

Eyes   Super Pearl ¼ 3D Adhesive Eyes (OP4-367)

SCHMIDT'S RED ROCKET TYING INSTRUCTIONS

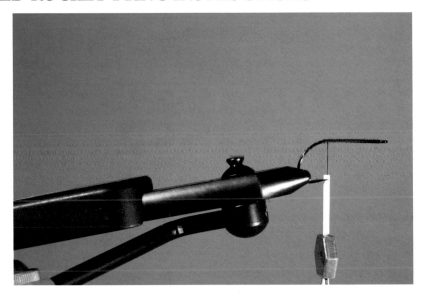

Step 1   With your Gamakatsu B-10s size 2 hook in the vise, get some Black UTC 140 or Veevus 6/0 thread started and wrapped to the back of the hook shank.

Step 2   Once at the rear tie-in point, located above the midpoint of the hook spear, tie in Hareline Dubbin Inc. Tan Rabbit Zonker Strip off the back of the hook. The strip should hang off the back about 1–1½ inches. Once it is securely in place, tie in and trim Hedron Inc. Holographic Gold Flashabou so that it sticks out just a bit past the rabbit.

Step 3 At the rear tie-in point, attach a single Hareline Dubbin Inc. Yellow Schlappen Feather by the tip and then the Hareline Dubbin Inc. Large Root Beer Cactus Chenille with a few tight wraps each, then advance the thread forward to the eye. Wrap the cactus chenille forward to form the underbody of the fly.

Step 4 Palmer the schlappen forward and tie it off. Be careful as you wrap forward not to trap fibers down to the body.

Step 5   Just behind the eye finish the back of the fly by tying in a marabou veil using Hareline Dubbin Inc. Tan Marabou Blood Quill. The marabou tips should extend past the schlappen and about half way down the rabbit strip.

Step 6   Tie in two pairs of Hareline Dubbin Inc. Speckled Pumpkin Crazy Legs so they come down each side of the hook shank and trim them so they extend about to the bend of the hook. Whip-finish the rear hook.

Step 7   For the front hook, place a Gamakatsu B-10s size 1 hook in the vise. Attach the rear hook using 3 inches of Hareline Dubbin Inc. Trailer Hook Wire threaded through the eye with two 3mm Red Glass beads as spacers. Tightly wrap crossing wraps forward and back to lock the connection in place.

Step 8   Using another six to ten strands of Hedron Inc. Holographic Gold Flashabou you will form a skirt off the back of the front hook to add internal flash and help cover the junction. Tie them in by the middle on one side of the hook shank and then fold them back over themselves and tie them off. They should extend about to the back of the schlappen on the rear hook.

Step 9   At the rear tie in point you now attach a single schlappen feather by the tip and then the cactus chenille with a few tight wraps each, then advance the thread forward to the eye. Wrap the cactus chenille forward to form the underbody of the fly.

Step 10   Palmer the schlappen forward and tie it off. You should leave about ¼–⅓ inch behind the eye for the remaining steps.

Step 11   Tie in a marabou veil as previously. The marabou tips should extend past the schlappen and extend over the junction point.

Step 12   Tie in two Hareline Dubbin Inc. Speckled Pumpkin Crazy Legs so they come down each side of the hook shank and trim them so they extend about to the bend of the front hook.

Step 13   Over the tie-in point for the legs you will add the Natural Grizzly Mini Marabou cheeks. The cheeks will extend about the length of the hook shank, so just short of the rubber legs.

Step 14   Form the throat by tying in Senyo's Pink Lady Fusion Dub.

Step 15   Form the head by tying in a clump of Senyo's Tan Laser Dub over the top of the throat.

Step 16   Using Loctite, glue in Super Pearl ¼ 3D Adhesive Eyes on either side of the hook.

31

Justin's S.B.E.
(Swim Bait Envy)

With over ten full seasons chasing striped bass in the northeast, the effectiveness of Popovic's hollow fly was clear. The entire fly breathes and pulses, offering a fuller profile that seems to get the bigger, smarter game fish we all want to get our hands on. The fact that hollow flies are just fun to observe and fish was maybe the main reason for tying the S.B.E., though. Similar patterns work well for pike and musky but the hook is often too big, or the tail too long for other freshwater game fish. By stretching the body of the fly over a shank and adding a rear hook, this provided a versatile crossover streamer that provided the big profile, pulsing body, and ease of casting I found so effective in the hollow fly. The S.B.E. will dart and wiggle like many common articulated flies today, with the addition of a large, full-bodied profile that breathes and wiggles whether stripped or on the pause. The S.B.E. can be fished wading with a floating or intermediate line, or intermediate or sinking line by boat. Big strips and pauses are effective but read the fly and how fish respond. You can burn it over flats two-handed or dredge it deep with a slow, single-handed strip and big pauses. With any streamer, reading the fish maybe as important as anything. If a fish shows on a certain retrieve like the big strip-and-pause, they liked something. Keep it going, or give it one more big strip-and-pause and keep it coming with more kicks and pauses with less time in between. Reading the fish pays off. If fish are reluctant to strike when sped up, a slower, deeper presentation over the same or similar area can produce.

The fish mask offers a versatile, neutral buoyancy head, but this pattern is more of a template like many common streamers today. Deer-hair heads are also effective, or big bead chain similar to a Whistler help get the fly down and will add some up-and-down movement. The big stainless bead chain eyes will also add a durable rattle to the fly.

Target Species   Brown trout, musky, pike, and bass

Favorite Color Combinations   Olive/White/Yellow, Olive/Pink/White, Brown/Tan/Yellow, Black/Chart/Orange, Black/Purple and Black/Olive.

JUSTIN'S SWIM BAIT ENVY MATERIALS

Thread   Black 150 Veevus GSP (150G-11)

Rear Hook   Gamakatsu B-10S Size 2

Shoulder   Hareline Dubbin Inc. Black Northern Bucktail (NB-11)

Flash   Hedron Inc. Holographic Purple Flashabou (HFL-6999)

Tail   Hareline Dubbin Inc. Black Strung Saddle Hackle (SCSD-11)

Tail 2   Hareline Dubbin Inc. Purple Strung Saddle Hackle (SCSD-298)

Body   Hareline Dubbin Inc. Senyo's Mixed Berries Aqua Veil Chenille (SA-4)

Wing   Hareline Dubbin Inc. Black Northern Bucktail (NB-11)

Body 2   Hareline Dubbin Inc. Senyo's Mixed Berries Aqua Veil Chenille (SA-4)

Top Collar   Hareline Dubbin Inc. Black Northern Bucktail (NB-11)

Shank   20mm Flymen Fishing Company Articulated Fish Spine (20FS)

Body   Hareline Dubbin Inc. Senyo's Mixed Berries Aqua Veil Chenille (SA-4)

Collar   Hareline Dubbin Inc. Black Northern Bucktail (NB-11)

Wire   Hareline Dubbin Inc. Trailer Hook Wire (THW-165)

Beads   6mm Silver Pro Eye Beads

Front Hook   Gamakatsu B-10S Hook size 1/0

Flash   Hedron Inc. Holographic Purple Flashabou (HFL-6999)

Body   Hareline Dubbin Inc. Senyo's Mixed Berries Aqua Veil (SA-4)

Under Wing   Hareline Dubbin Inc. Black Northern Bucktail (NB-11)

Body 2   Hareline Dubbin Inc. Senyo's Mixed Berries Aqua Veil Chenille (SA-4)

Top Wing   Hareline Dubbin Inc. Black Northern Bucktail (NB-11)

Flash   Hedron Inc. Holographic Purple Flashabou (HFL-6999)

Collar   EP Senyo's 3.0 Midnight Chromatic Brush (WSC-11)

Head   Flymen Fishing Company Fish Skull Fish Mask Size 7 (FFm-7)

Eyes   Red Eye 5/16 3D Adhesive Eyes (OP5-310)

Glue   Loctite Gel

JUSTIN'S SWIM BAIT ENVY TYING INSTRUCTIONS

Step 1   Tie in a shoulder of Hareline Dubbin Inc. Black Northern Bucktail on a Gamakatsu B-10s Size 2 hook using Black 150 Veevus GSP thread.

Step 2   Tie in some Hedron Inc. Holographic Purple Flashabou at the bend of the rear hook. This can be prepared parachute-posted or coated with clear cure goo to prevent fouling and increase durability.

Step 3   Tie in two matching Hareline Dubbin Inc. Black Strung Saddle Hackle feathers.

Step 4 Tie in two more Hareline Dubbin Inc. Purple Strung Saddle Hackle feathers.

Step 5 Tie in a strip of Hareline Dubbin Inc. Senyo's Mixed Berries Aqua Veil Chenille and wrap half way up the hook shank.

Step 6   Reverse-tie a clump of Hareline Dubbin Inc. Black Northern Bucktail. This is the first of two sections. The first is shortest, increasing in length each time.

Step 7   Repeat steps 5 and 6. Whip-finish the tail section.

Step 8   Create the middle section by using a 4-inch piece of Hareline Dubbin Inc. Trailer Hook Wire that will connect the rear hook to the front hook. For the front hook, use a 1/0 Gamakatsu B-10s hook. Use two 6mm Silver Pro Eye Beads to slip over the wire before connecting to the front hook. Secure the wire with several thread wraps over the shank of your front hook.

Step 9   Tie in a clump of Hedron Inc. Holographic Purple Flashabou to cover the connection point.

Step 10   Tie in a strip of Hareline Dubbin Inc. Senyo's Mixed Berries Aqua Veil and make three or four turns of up the hook shank, carefully stroking the fibers toward the rear of the hook as your wrap.

Step 11   Reverse-tie a clump of Hareline Dubbin Inc. Black Northern Bucktail, followed by more Mixed Berries Aqua Veil Chenille, wrapped three or four times.

Step 12   Reverse-tie another clump of Black Northern Bucktail or alternate the color to match the fly.

Step 13   Tie in a lateral line using Holographic Purple Flashabou, running down both sides of the fly.

Step 14   Tie in 3 inches of EP Senyo's 3.0 Midnight Chromatic Brush for remainder of hook shank and collar.

Step 15   Slide over the hook eye, a Flymen Fishing Company Fish Skull Fish Mask Size 7 and using Loctite, glue in one Red Eye 5/16 3D Adhesive Eye to both sides of the Fish Mask. *Note:* Can be tied in various sizes and colors to meet a lot of needs for trout, bass, pike and small and medium musky fly. Switch the back hook to a shank and works well in the northeast salt.

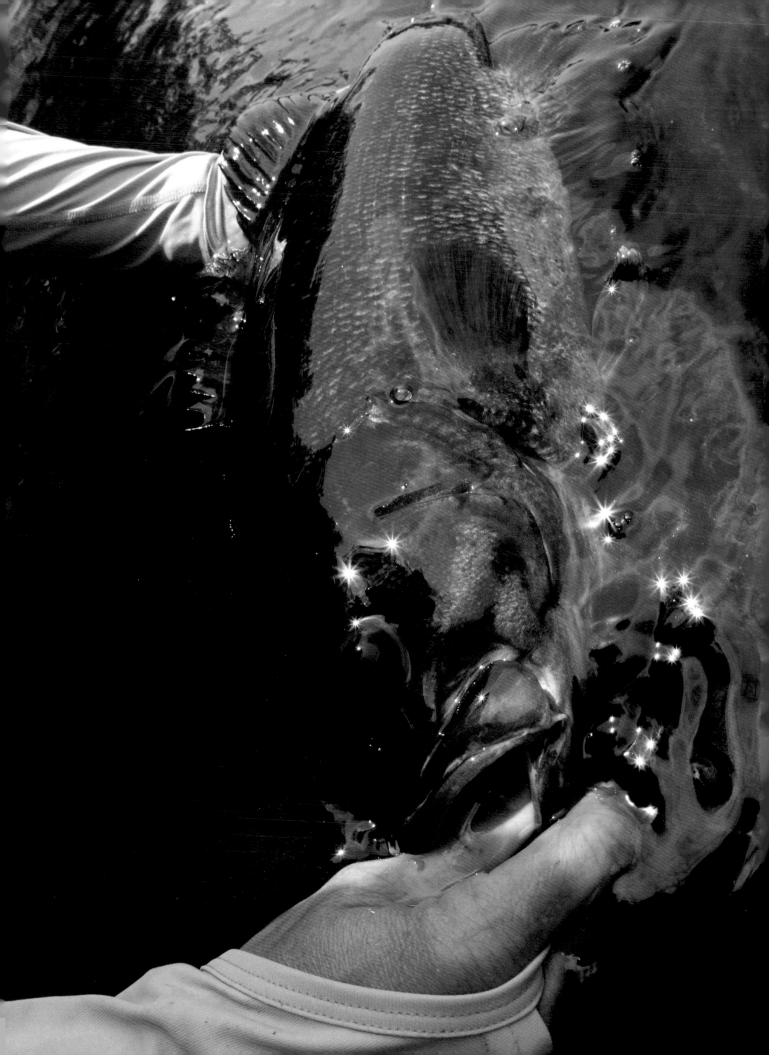

32

HUGHES'S WILD BILL

There are a lot of great tiers out there. Guys who create innovative patterns that do more than just catch fishermen, they also catch fish. I've been lucky enough to meet, work, and fish with some of these characters over the last few years, and I'm proud to say that they have taught me more in that short time than I could have learned in dozens on my own. They've dragged me into a world of large streamers, new-age materials, and flies that get killed rather than just eaten.

I personally do not consider this pattern to be anything new, but more of a variation upon a theme that's been kicking around for some time now.

Swapping out some old for some new, tweaking this or that, and fiddling with weight distribution and profile to get a desired swimming action. The pattern remains light, it rattles, flashes, kicks, and subsequently dies with each pause in the retrieve. All things I consider important when throwing this fly (or others) when fishing for smallmouth bass and other game species.

Hughes's Wild Bill is an easy-casting, lightweight streamer with a proven "kick-and-die" swimming action. Thanks to extensive use of synthetic materials, it is a durable fly that is quick and easy to tie. It's best fished on an intermediate line with a strip-and-pause retrieve.

Target Species   Resident trout, bass, walleye, and pike

Favorite Color Combinations   White, Black, Rust, Chartreuse, Olive, Tan, Yellow, Brown

HUGHES'S WILD BILL MATERIALS

Thread   Black UTC 140 or Veevus 6/0 (6V-11)

Rear Hook   Gamakatsu Worm Hook Size 1/0

Shoulder   Hareline Dubbin Inc. White Northern Bucktail (NB-377)

Tail   Hareline Dubbin Inc. Chartreuse Strung Saddle Hackle (SCSD-54)

Flash   Hedron Inc. Holographic Chartreuse Flashabou (HFL-3289)

Body   Hareline Dubbin Inc. Senyo's Nuked Green Bean Aqua Veil Chenille (SA-6)

Hackle   EP Senyo 1.5 Live Bait Chromatic Brush (SCB-9)

Bottom Collar   Hareline Dubbin Inc. White Northern Bucktail (NB-377)

Top Collar   Hareline Dubbin Inc. Chartreuse Northern Bucktail (NB-54)

Wire   Hareline Dubbin Inc. Trailer Hook Wire (THW-165)

Beads   6mm Green Pro Eye Beads

Front Hook   Gamakatsu Worm Hook size 2/0

Flash   Hedron Inc. Holographic Chartreuse Flashabou (HFL-3289)

Body   Hareline Dubbin Inc. Senyo's Nuked Green Bean Aqua Veil (SA-6)

Rattle   5mm Glass (RAT-5)

Hackle   EP Senyo 3.0 Live Bait Chromatic Brush (WSC-9)

Bottom Collar   Hareline Dubbin Inc. White Northern Bucktail (NB-377)

Top Collar   Hareline Dubbin Inc. Chartreuse Northern Bucktail (NB-54)

Flash 1   Hedron Inc. Holographic Chartreuse Flashabou (HFL-3289)

Flash 2   Senyo's UV Barred Predator Wrap (BPW-2)

Head   Enrico Puglisi Minnow Gray UV Minnow Head Brush (MHB-7)

Eyes   Super Pearl ¼ 3D Adhesive Eyes (OP4-367)

HUGHES'S WILD BILL TYING INSTRUCTIONS

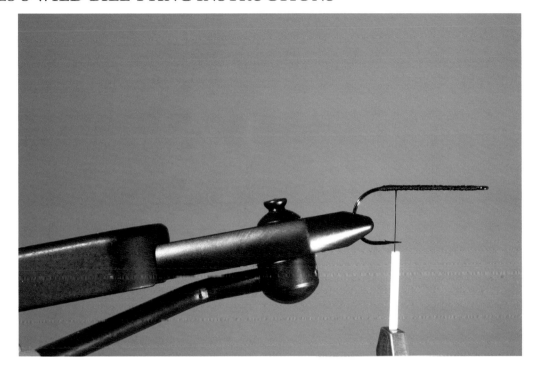

Step 1   Starting with the rear hook, use a Gamakatsu Worm Hook Size 1/0 and lay down a Black UTC 140 or Veevus 6/0 thread base the entire length of the hook.

Step 2   Tie in a small clump of Hareline Dubbin Inc. White Northern Bucktail, about the length of the hook shank. This will serve as a base for the tail that will also double as a foul guard for your tail feathers later.

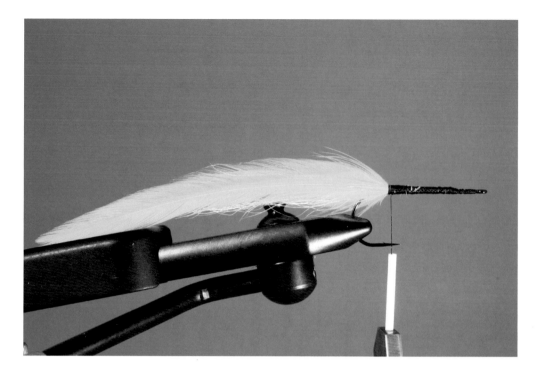

Step 3 Continue to create the tail by tying two Hareline Dubbin Inc. Chartreuse Strung Saddle Hackle feathers so the curves face each other (concave sides facing each other), one on either side of the hook, so they run alongside the bucktail. The saddle feathers should extend about 4 inches off the back of the hook.

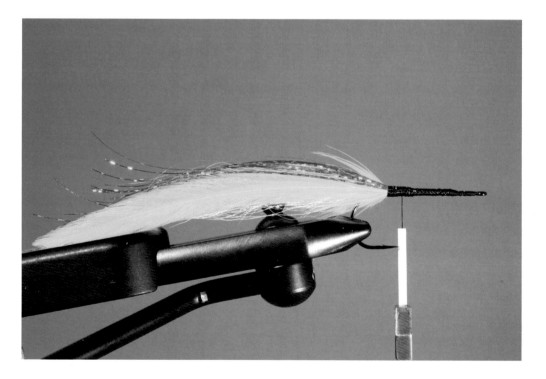

Step 4 Tie in Hedron Inc. Holographic Chartreuse Flashabou over top of tail feathers so the flash extends just to the tips of the feather.

Step 5   Tie in about 4 inches of Hareline Dubbin Inc. Senyo's Nuked Green Bean Aqua Veil Chenille and evenly wrap toward the front of the shank and secure with several thread wraps, stopping about ¼ inch from the hook eye. As you wrap, stroke the fibers toward the rear of the hook.

Step 6   Tie in EP Senyo 1.5 Live Bait Chromatic Brush, make three wraps to tie in the throat and tie off. Brush out the fibers to release any that have become trapped while wrapping.

Step 7   Take one clump of Chartreuse Northern Bucktail (about a quarter of a pencil) and tie in on top of shank. The bucktail should be about 1½ times the length of the hook shank. Take a second clump of white bucktail about the same size and secure it to the bottom of the hook.

Step 8   Create the wire junction to the front hook by threading a 6-inch piece of Hareline Dubbin Inc. Trailer Hook Wire through the eye of the rear hook and doubling it over. Slide two 6mm Green Pro Eye Beads over the doubled wire. Wire should run along the side of the front hook shank, and the loop created should be slightly vertical, allowing the rear hook to swing from side to side during the retrieve.

Step 9   At the rear of the front hook (Gamakatsu Worm Hook size 2/0), tie in a clump of Holographic Chartreuse Flashabou to cover the wire connection.

Step 10   Tie in about 4 inches of Senyo's Nuked Green Bean Aqua Veil at the same point as the flashabou. At the same junction, tie in the 5mm Glass rattle, keeping it close to the tie-in point of the Aqua Veil and flashabou. I have found that fixing the rattle this far back on this pattern gives the fly a better action than if you were to position it farther up the shank. For additional security, consider a light coating of Clear Cure Goo over the thread wraps surrounding the rattle, and curing it with a UV light.

Step 11   Advance thread towards the eye of the hook, and wrap the Aqua Veil, palmering over the rattle. Stop about ¾ inch from the hook eye and tie off.

Step 12   Tie in EP Senyo 3.0 Live Bait Chromatic Brush. Make three wraps and tie off.

Step 13   Tie in another pinch (about half a pencil in thickness) of Chartreuse Northern Bucktail on top of hook. Bucktail should extend past the connection to the rear hook, approximately two times the length of the hook shank. Tie in white bucktail underneath hook equal to the length of the bucktail on the top and tied in the same spot.

Step 14   Take Senyo's UV Barred Predator Wrap and cut off fifteen to twenty strands from the string and tie the strands on top of the hook shank along with a mix of Holographic Chartreuse Flashabou and lateral scale. This adds more dimension to fly, giving it the illusion of scale pattern.

Step 15   Tie in Enrico Puglisi Minnow Gray UV Minnow Head Brush and wrap forward, stopping just behind the eye. Whip finish and brush out the head to release any fibers that have become trapped while wrapping the head. Glue in Super Pearl ¼ 3D Adhesive Eyes, then coat eyes and nose of the fly with Clear Cure Goo or Loon Flow. Harden with UV light.

33

MT Minnow

This streamer can be tied in many different color combinations and in various degrees of weight. This updated Fish Skull version will give the fly a slight side-to-side action, and a jigging action with a stripped hand line. This pattern has become a favorite trout streamer on the Delaware River after ice-out in early spring for brown trout, and a good option for high water on the Great Lakes tributaries for steelhead. I've adapted this pattern from my older version, which used two hooks and lead eyes, in favor of a Fish Skull, articulated shank, and a single stinger hook. I have found this to be much more productive catch ratio and less likely to leave the fly snagged along the river bottom. The hooks tend to bend out, making for easy replacement before the fly can be lost for good.

Target Species   Resident and migratory trout, and Great Lakes steelhead

Favorite Color Combinations   Chartreuse/Pearl, Olive/Pearl (Rainbow Trout), Brown/Orange (Brown trout), Gray/Pearl (Shad)

MT MINNOW MATERIALS

Shank   40mm Copper Senyo Flymen Fishing Company Articulated Salmon/Steelhead Shank (40SA-271)

Wire   Hareline Dubbin Inc. Senyo Intruder Wire or 30-pound Berkley Original Fused Fireline (THW-165)

Thread   Veevus white 6/0 (6V-377)

Tail   Hareline Dubbin Inc. Light Brown and Black Barred Rabbit Zonker Strip (BRS-205)

Body   Hareline Dubbin Inc. UV Gold Polar Chenille (PCUV-153)

Thorax   Hareline Dubbin Inc. Ice Dub UV Pearl (ICE-285)

Thorax 2   Hareline Dubbin Inc. UV Hot Orange Ice Dub (ICE-187)

Wing   Hareline Dubbin Inc. Light Brown and Black Barred Rabbit Zonker Strip (BRS-205)

Flash   Six to eight Strands Speckled Copper Flashabou (FLM-6934)

Head   Medium Flymen Fishing Company Copper Tone Fish Skull (FKM-67)

Eyes   Flymen Fishing Company 3mm Fire Living Eyes (3LE-3)

MT MINNOW TYING INSTRUCTIONS

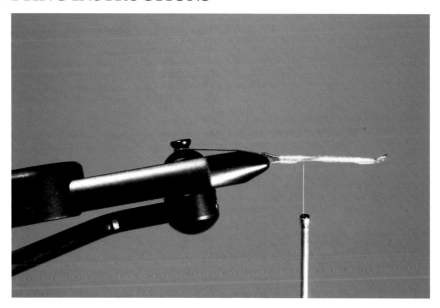

Step 1   Place a copper 40mm Senyo Steelhead Shank from Flymen Fishing Company in your vise. Attach your UTC 70 or Veevus 6/0 thread and evenly coat the entire shank and close both front and rear loops with a thin base of thread. Cut off a 4-inch piece of Senyo's Intruder Wire or 30-pound Berkley Fireline and secure it to both sides of the shank with several thread wraps. Take the tag ends through the bottom of the front loop and fold over the top of the shank. Pull tight over the top of the shank and tie down securely with several even thread wraps. Adding glue for strength is optional. Your wire loop length should not exceed 2 inches in total length.

Step 2   Tie in a 5-inch long piece of Olive/black barred rabbit zonker strip, so that approximately 2½ inches sticks out the rear as the tail. The rest of the rabbit zonker strip will become the wing in another step, just fold it over the hook out of the way.

Step 3 Tie in a 4-inch piece of UV Gold Polar Chenille and palmer an even body forward stopping where the two wires come together to form the eye of the shank.

Step 4 Take and center tie a small clump of Hareline's UV pearl ice dubbing to form the under belly of the fly pattern.

Step 5   Next take a sparse clump of Hareline's UV Hot Orange colored Ice Dub and tie in over the pearl so that an even amount of ice dub is visible on each side of the head.

Step 6   Grab and pull over the piece of black barred rabbit strip over the top and center it over the polar chenille and ice dubbing. Pull tight on the rabbit strip and secure with several thread wraps.

Step 7   Add six to eight Strands of Copper speckled flashabou over top of the rabbit strip wing. Take your copper Fish Skull and place a pair 3mm Fire colored living eyes in the sockets. Add a drop of Loctite to the top of the shank and slide on the skull until it is snug against the materials. Cut your thread and allow to dry.

34

FEATHER GAME CHANGER

Being a successful fly fisherman and fly tier means you have to be observant, persistent and be able to think outside of the box. Blane Chocklett patterns are almost always a crossover between swimbait lures and streamer flies. The Game Changer, in particular, is an articulated streamer pattern that encompasses all of his innovation, and is a great example of Fusion Fly Tying at its best. Blane has brought many new concepts and materials to the fly tying community, but perhaps his most influential pattern is the Game Changer, which uses a synthetic material such as Minnow Wrap.

The Feather Game Changer is an adaptation of Blane's original Game Changer and also series of wire shanks of varying sizes, but is tied completely with feathers, making this fly versatile in color, size, and cleans up for predatory fish species such as trout, bass, musky, and pike. It's also light and easy to cast.

Experimenting with hen saddle wrapped around the shanks, the Feathered Game Changer is still dense enough to move water while being stripped, but can easily be adjusted in size to meet the appearance of large sculpins as well as another of other bait fish with just a change of feather color. With quick start-and-stop retrieves, the feathers swell and flow naturally in the water, and add that great suspending pause which is a perfect trigger for predatory fish. Fish this fly on an intermediate or sinking line for best results as that will keep the fly just below the surface, or sink to a deeper depth of your choosing.

Target Species   Resident trout, bass, walleye, and pike

Favorite Color Combinations   White, Black, Chartreuse, Olive, Tan, Yellow, Brown, Clowned (Mixed Colors)

FEATHER GAME CHANGER MATERIALS

Thread   Chartreuse UTC 140 or Veevus 6/0 (6V-143)

Rear shank   Flymen Fishing Company 10mm articulated Fish Spine (10FS)

Tail   Hareline Dubbin Inc. Grizzly Mini Marabou (GRIZM247)

Collar   Hareline Dubbin Inc. Grizzly Hen feathers (1MHS-176)

Shank 2   Flymen Fishing Company 15mm articulated Fish Spine (15FS)

Body   Hareline Dubbin Inc. Grizzly Hen Feathers (1MHS-176)

Shank 3   Flymen Fishing Company 20mm articulated Fish Spine (20FS)

Body   Hareline Dubbin Inc. Grizzly Hen Feathers (1MHS-176)

Shank 4   Flymen Fishing Company 25mm articulated Fish Spine (25FS)

Body   Hareline Dubbin Inc. Grizzly Hen Feathers (1MHS-176)

Wire   Hareline Dubbin Inc. Trailer Hook Wire (THW-165)

Front Hook   Partridge Attitude Extra 2/0

Body   Hareline Dubbin Inc. Grizzly Hen Feathers (1MHS-176)

Fins   Hareline Dubbin Inc. Grizzly Saddle Feather (1MHS-176)

Head   Hareline Dubbin Inc. Grizzly Saddle Feather (1MHS-176)

FEATHER GAME CHANGER TYING INSTRUCTIONS

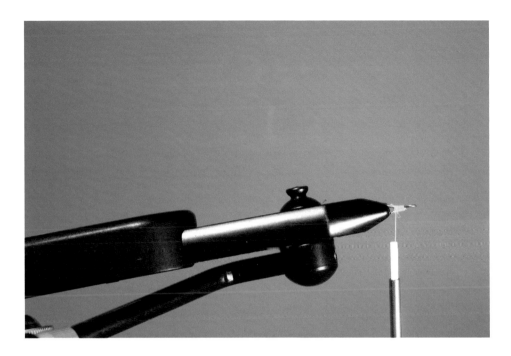

Step 1   Place a Flymen Fishing Company 10mm articulated Fish Spine in your vise. Use pliers to break the shank at the apex of the bend, or cut it with wire cutters. Start the thread behind the eye and build an even layer base of Chartreuse UTC 140 or Veevus 6/0.

Step 2   Tie in a tail of Hareline Dubbin Inc. Grizzly Mini Marabou

Step 3   Follow this with a body of wrapped Grizzly Hen feathers. Wrap to the eye and tie down. Connect a 15mm articulated Fish Spine to the tail and place the 15mm shank in the vise.

Step 4   Tie in a body of wrapped Grizzly Hen feathers. Increase the size of the feather as you progress up the shank. Wrap to the eye and tie down. Connect a 20mm articulated Fish Spine to the 15mm shank. Place the 20mm shank in the vise. Secure the thread wraps on the 20mm shank, stopping at the apex of the bend. Tie in a body of wrapped Grizzly Hen feathers. Increase the size of the feather as you progress in the size of the shank. Wrap to the eye and tie down. The more feathers you can wrap on the shank, the better it will swim. Connect a 25mm articulated Fish Spine to the 20mm shank. Place the 25mm shank in the vise. Secure the thread wraps on the 25mm shank, stopping at the apex of the bend. Tie in a body of wrapped Grizzly Hen feathers. Increase the size of the feather as you progress in the size of the shank. Wrap to the eye and tie down.

Step 5   Insert the Partridge Attitude Extra 2/0 hook in the vise and wrap a thread base slightly down the bend. Make the connection between the 25mm shank and the hook using Hareline Dubbin Inc. Trailer Hook Wire or monofilament. Wrap the thread over the wire toward the hook bend. Run the wire through the eye of the 25mm shank, fold it over, and wrap over the remaining wire on the hook shank.

Step 6   Tie in a body of wrapped Grizzly Hen feathers on the hook. Increase the size of the feather as you progress in the size of the shank. Wrap to the eye and tie down. The more feathers you can wrap on the shank, the better it will swim.

Step 7   Add in the pectoral fins using Grizzly Hen Saddle on either side. Tie in one or two feathers on either side so they splay out, similar to the head of a sculpin.

Step 8   Tie in one or two more Grizzly Hen Saddle Feathers and wrap to finish the head.

35

STROLIS'S BUSH MEAT STREAMER

The Bushmeat streamer resulted from the necessity of another sculpin variation for my streamer addiction. Sometimes, having something a little different than the ordinary pattern will save the day when the fishing gets tough, and my creative side is always looking for something fresh. My thoughts were to devise a pattern that was constructed almost entirely of synthetic materials that had similar movement to a fly built out of copious amounts of arctic fox or rabbit fur. Although this fly uses a foxy brush, which has arctic fox in its construction, the brush itself is a 75/25 split of synthetic to fox so essentially it is nearly all synthetic so to speak.

I have a tendency to fish streamers a great deal every season, and sculpin imitations are some of the patterns I fish the most. Trout have a propensity to feast on this forage as they are not the most agile food forms available, and can provide a high-protein punch for any trout. What I like to incorporate in my sculpin imitations is not only bulk near the head of the fly, but also the addition of weight. The tungsten dumbbell gives this fly enough weight at the head, essentially creating more vertical action in the fly as opposed to just horizontal action provided by the articulation.

A great deal of my success fishing with sculpin imitations has hinged around this concept of up-and-down action reminiscent of a jig. This action can be further enhanced in the way that the fly is fished. An erratic strip and long pause cadence during the retrieve makes the fly move up and down in the water column, and if given the time to reach the streambed, it will act very much like the natural. Tying the dumbbell on the top of the hook inverts the fly in the water column, forcing the hook point to ride in the up position, drastically cutting down on snags and lost flies. Any sort of action imparted by the angler either through the rod or via the strip of the fly line will usually result in a violent take or stop of the line. If the fly stops, the line is jolted in your hand, or begins moving in any direction but downstream, strip set and hang on. What is very nice about this fly is if you keep a small wire dog comb in your vest you can comb out the fly after every fish bringing the fly back to shape. Synthetics have a tendency to tangle after prolonged use and a comb can rejuvenate them quickly.

Target Species   Brown trout and bass

Favorite Color Combinations   White, Black, Rust, Chartreuse, Olive, Tan, Yellow, Brown

STROLIS'S BUSH MEAT STREAMER MATERIALS

Thread   Brown UTC 140 or Veevus 6/0 (6V-323)

Rear Hook   Gamakatsu SP11-3L3H size 2

Flash   Senyo's UV Barred Predator Wrap (BPW-2)

Tail   Hareline Dubbin Inc. Dark Brown Extra Select Craft Fur (XCF-87)

Body   Hareline Dubbin Inc. Senyo's Peanut Brittle Aqua Veil (SA-7)

Wing   Hareline Dubbin Inc. Dark Brown Extra Select Craft Fur (XCF-87)

Wire   Hareline Dubbin Inc. Trailer Hook Wire (THW-11)

Beads   6mm Red Pro Eye bead

Front Hook   Gamakatsu B-10S size 1

Body   Hareline Dubbin Inc. Senyo's Peanut Brittle Aqua Veil (SA-7)

Wing   Hareline Dubbin Inc. Dark Brown Extra Select Craft Fur (XCF-87)

Flash   Senyo's UV Barred Predator Wrap (BPW-2)

Collar   Hareline Dubbin Inc. Senyo's Peanut Brittle Aqua Veil (SA-7)

Eyes   Hareline Dubbin Inc. Tungsten Predator Eyes (TPM-383)

Head   Enrico Puglisi Speckled Brown UV Minnow Head Brush (MHB-16)

STROLIS'S BUSH MEAT STREAMER TYING INSTRUCTIONS

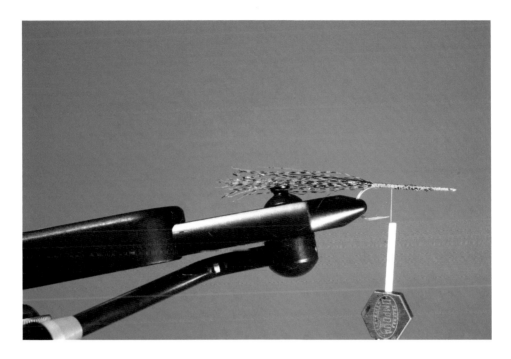

Step 1   Place the Gamakatsu SP11-3L3H size 2 hook in the vise and wrap Brown UTC 140 or Veevus 6/0 thread from the eye to the hook point. Cut six strands of Senyo's UV Barred Predator Wrap, tie in, taking two turns and fold the forward sections rearward securing them.

Step 2   Cut a pencil-sized section of Hareline Dubbin Inc. Dark Brown Extra Select Craft Fur, comb out the under fur and tie in, enveloping the predator wrap. The butt ends should extend to a point just behind the hook eye. Secure the craft fur with thread wraps and return your tying thread to the base of the tail.

Step 3   Tie in a section of Hareline Dubbin Inc. Senyo's Peanut Brittle Aqua Veil at that base of the tail and advance your thread to the hook eye. Wrap the aqua veil along the hook shank to approximately ⅛ inch from the hook eye and tie off.

Step 4   Cut a second pencil-sized section of Dark Brown Extra Select Craft Fur, comb out the under fur and reverse-tie the bundle at the front of the hook. Be sure to roll the bundle 360 degrees around the hook so that it will create an even wing. After ten to fifteen turns of thread, brush a small amount of Hydro Clear Cure Goo over the craft fur butt ends extending rearward and cure them with a UV light. Fold the craft fur extending forward over the hook eye rearward to make a wing that sunbursts around the hook, advancing your thread through the bundle. Whip finish and cement the thread wraps. The head should be bullet shaped.

Step 5 Thread a Hareline Dubbin Inc. Trailer Hook Wire through the eye of the completed rear section and add a 6mm Red Pro Eye bead. Thread the other end of the wire through the bead. Place the Gamakatsu B-10s size 1 hook in the vise and run a course of thread from the eye to the bend. Attach the rear hook to the front hook by tying down the wire along the front hook shank, being sure to keep both hooks running in the same direction.

Step 6 Figure eight tie the Hareline Dubbin Inc. Tungsten Predator Eyes to the top of the hook about 1 hook eyes length in front of the collar. Wrap your thread back to the rear of the hook and attach a section of Senyo's Peanut Brittle Aqua Veil and wrap it forward covering a third of the hook and tie it off.

Step 7 Cut a pencil-sized section of Dark Brown Extra Select Craft Fur and remove the under fur. Reverse-tie the bundle in the same manner as the front section of the rear hook but this time right at the rear where the wire connection meets the front hook. Apply clear cure goo hydro as this will build a small spreader to the connection.

Step 8 After securing the craft fur, add six strands of Senyo's UV Barred Predator Wrap and tie it in, enveloping the craft fur.

Step 9   Tie in a collar of Senyo's Peanut Brittle Aqua Veil over the predator wrap and wrap it forward to just behind the eyes and tie off.

Step 10   Tie in Enrico Puglisi Speckled Brown UV Minnow Head Brush behind the dumbbell eyes. Make two turns behind the eyes, then figure eight the brush through the top and bottom of the dumbbell eyes making two more turns behind the eyes before making two turns in front. Secure the brush and whip finish. Brush out the head and collar with a small wire comb or dog brush.

36

LARIMER ARTICULATED CRAW BUGGER

I'm obsessed with the fusion of spey casting and trout fishing. Although I love single-handed casting and fishing, spey rods offer a new challenge in the trout game. Plus, it's easy to fall in love with spey casting because it's so incredibly fun! Outside of the casting, I've discovered that microspey rods are unbelievably effective tools for a wide range of trout fishing techniques. However, my favorite way to fish the little two-handers is to swing streamers.

Over the years of chasing trout with spey rods I've realized that while traditional streamers do work, I was missing a lot of fish. Through a lot of trial and error I've come to the conclusion that a trout, especially a rainbow trout, eats a swinging fly differently than a streamer that is cast at the bank and stripped. They often nip at the tail and miss the hook. Consequently, I felt the need for trout patterns designed specifically for swing fishing. I wanted to take the concept of "stinger" style patterns used for steelheading and incorporate it into my trout streamers.

Almost twenty years ago a friend of mine showed me a nondescript bugger style pattern developed by a guide named Tim Holschlag called the "Holschlag Hackle Fly" that he had been using to crush smallmouth. Essentially it was a brown bugger with some copper flash in the tail, yellow legs and red dumbbell eyes. It was nothing special. That said, the first day I threw it on a trout river made me realize the simple pattern had some serious juju… The trout went crazy over it! Given my success, my friend urged me to try the fly with an olive body. They worked as well or at times even better than the brown version. This pattern no doubt influenced my time at the vise when creating the Articulated Bugger.

When I first started working on the Articulated Bugger I had a few requirements. First off, I was looking for a swing pattern that could be hopped like a fleeing crawfish. Secondly, I wanted to use a small stinger hook near the rear of the fly for those short taking grabs. I played around with a stinger hook on a wire loop but always found the tail wrapped around it and fouled the fly. While the stinger loop has its place, it didn't work well for this pattern. Instead, I tied a short, bugger style tail with rabbit and crystal flash on an egg hook, which forms the rear half of the fly. This alone brought the hook-up and landing ratio way up when compared to a traditional streamer hook. More so, I wanted the fly to breathe life while under tension. Outside of a marabou tail, a standard bugger has no movement within the body. I opted for a spun rabbit body on the front half of the pattern to create seductive movement even in light current. I've also realized that the bulky front half pushes the water as it swings. Not only does this help move the tail by creating a vortex within the fly, it also creates an audible footprint that trout can pick up on their lateral line. Finally, I wanted to incorporate the yellow legs and red eyes of the Holschlag Hackle Fly. I've found that medium-sized eyes work great if I want to hop the pattern during the swing to imitate a crawfish. However, I will dress the fly with smaller eyes for slow, shallow rivers.

Since its development, the Articulated Bugger has become a mainstay in my trout spey box. I tie it in a number of other colors including olive, white, and dark brown. That being said, it's easy to come up with a wide range of color combinations for different fishing conditions. It can be tied to match a specific food source or as a general searching pattern. Like its traditional cousin, the Articulated Bugger is that fly that looks like nothing and everything all at the same time. More importantly, trout, smallmouth, and even steelhead love to crush it on the swing.

Target Species   Trout, steelhead, and bass

Favorite Color Combinations   White, Black, Rust, Chartreuse, Olive, Tan, Yellow, Brown

LARIMER ARTICULATED CRAW BUGGER MATERIALS

Thread   Brown UTC 140 or Veevus 6/0 (6V-323)

Rear Hook   Daiichi Short Shank Straight Eye Hook Size 6 (D1640-6)

Flash   Copper Krystal Flash (KF-8)

Tail   Hareline Dubbin Inc. Crawfish Rabbit Zonker Strip (RS-19)

Body   Hareline Dubbin Inc. Senyo's Crusty Nail Fusion Dub (FUS-1)

Rib   Ultra Wire Copper (UWS-67)

Hackle   Hareline Dubbin Inc. Fiery Brown Saddle Feather (SCSD-114)

Wire   Hareline Dubbin Inc. Trailer Hook Wire (THW-165)

Beads   3mm Red Glass bead

Front Hook   Daiichi Short Shank Straight Eye Hook Size 6 (D1640-6)

Eyes   Medium Red Painted Lead (PLEM-310)

Body   Hareline Dubbin Inc. Crawfish Rabbit Zonker Strip (RS-19)

Rubber Legs   Hareline Dubbin Inc. Yellow Grizzly Barred Rubber Legs (GRM-383)

Collar   Hareline Dubbin Inc. Crawfish Rabbit Zonker Strip (RS-19)

Note   I tie this fly in olive, dark brown and white as well. I also tie it on size 8–10 hooks, usually with a bead chain eye for shallower, slower rivers.

LARIMER ARTICULATED CRAW BUGGER TYING INSTRUCTIONS

Step 1   Wrap Brown UTC 140 or Veevus 6/0 thread back to the bend of the Daiichi Short Shank Straight Eye Hook Size 6 hook. Tie in Copper Krystal Flash, by folding the crystal flash around the thread and wrapping the thread around the hook.

Step 2   Tie in clipped Hareline Dubbin Inc. Crawfish Rabbit Zonker Strip, with the majority of guard hairs removed.

Step 3   Tie in Ultra Wire Copper which will be used to segment the body after tying in the dubbing and hackle in the next steps. Dub a body of Hareline Dubbin Inc. Senyo's Crusty Nail Fusion Dub to just behind the eye of the hook. Make sure to taper the body as you advance the dubbing along the hook. Tie in a Hareline Dubbin Inc. Fiery Brown Saddle Feather by the stem at the point where you ended your dubbed body.

Step 4   Make three consecutive turns of hackle at the tie in point, then palmer toward the rear of the hook, ending where you tied in the copper wire. Wrap the copper wire forward, in the opposite direction of the hackle, to secure the hackle. Whip finish over the wire to complete the rear hook and trim the tag end of the hackle at the rear of the hook.

Step 5   Cut a 10-inch piece of Hareline Dubbin Inc. Trailer Hook Wire and thread wire through the rear hook eye and slide 3mm Red Glass bead. Place a Daiichi Short Shank Straight Eye Size 6 hook into your vise and wrap thread to the bend of the hook. Tie in Medium Red Painted Lead just behind the hook eye on the underside of the hook. Advance the thread to the rear of the hook to tie in the wire, and attach the rear hook to the front hook. Hold one piece of the wire at a slight angle up, wrap thread to the back of the hook, and then secure wire up to the eyes. Wrap the second piece of wire in the opposite directions around the base of the eyes and secure.

Step 6   In a dubbing loop, spin and dub two separate portions of clipped Hareline Dubbin Inc. Crawfish Rabbit Zonker Strip, leaving a 1-inch gap between the two clumps in the loop. Wrap the first clump of rabbit forward ending slightly forward of half way and take a couple of more wraps to secure. Following the next step, where you will tie in Hareline Dubbin Inc. Yellow Grizzly Barred Rubber legs, you will use the second clump of rabbit so be sure to leave yourself enough thread for securing the rubber legs.

Step 7   Tie in rubber legs by folding two legs around the thread. Move the legs up the thread to the hook and tie in, making sure to divide the legs evenly on both sides of the hook.

Step 8   Continue wrapping the rabbit dubbing loop to just behind the eyes and secure. Whip finish behind the eyes for maximum durability.

ACKNOWLEDGEMENTS

If I could turn back time and go back to the very beginning, you would be hard pressed to say I did anything as an individual. The truth is I always had someone to help push me forward. There has always been someone to pick me up off the dirt and dust me off. These individuals remained positive influences that helped me reach difficult goals in my life. I can easily say I owe you all a debt of gratitude for believing in me and excepting my small contribution to the fly fishing world. I am truly humbled that this small town boy from Girard, Pennsylvania was able to turn a lifelong dream into reality.

I would like to thank so many legendary, guides, tiers, companies, and local talents for influencing my tying, opening my mind, and making this book what it is. Shawn Brillon of the Orvis Company, a man who knows more about tying flies than anyone I know. Shawn was never afraid to tell me the truth, and was always willing to put others before himself. Marcos Vergara and Hareline Dubbin Inc. A mastermind behind anything and everything fly tying. Without his insight and support I'm not sure where I'd be today. Tom Larimer of Larimer Outfitters, for being an open book and sharing technical info and ideas based off your personal experiences with steelhead and salmon. Jerry French of Olympic Peninsula Skagit Tactics, for pushing the envelope in new fly tying techniques and synthetic pattern adaptions. Ed Ward of Olympic Peninsula Skagit Tactics, whose intruder fly pattern was the single most effective and creative steelhead fly pattern developed since the woolly bugger—a pattern that has sparked a tying revolution of new concepts and designs worldwide. Justin Pribanic, for creating and adapting patterns well before their time, and your open and willingness to put these concepts to the test both in theory and on the water. Kevin Feenstra of Feenstra Guide Services, for showing the Great Lakes the benefits of synthetic fly tying and pioneering and pushing fly design to the edge. Martin Bawden of Flymen Fishing Company, for realizing and giving me an opportunity to create new platforms and shanks to create functional fly patterns. Don Barnes of Regal Engineering, for providing me with the best quality vises and tools money can buy. John Miller, whose photography provide the excellent step by steps for this book, this project would not have been possible without your eyes behind the lens. Jay Wisnosky, for your willingness to be involved in this book behind the scenes since its inception and for making sure I stayed on task. Mike Schmidt, of Anglers Choice Flies for our incredible and entertaining tying sessions and numerous fly fishing adventures. Matt Supinski, noted author, guide, and steelhead/salmon maniac, thank you for inspiring me and opening doorways for the young anglers. You always remained a positive influence and voice that helped me stay true to myself and my passions. A big thanks to my editors Jay Cassell and Leah Zarra, and Tony Lyons for helping me through the publishing process. To everyone who helped contribute to this book, no matter how small, I am extremely grateful for everything you all have done.